THE

Church Revitalization Checklist

A Hopeful and Practical Guide

for Leading Your Congregation

to a Brighter Tomorrow

Sam Rainer

TYNDALE
MOMENTUM®

A Tyndale nonfiction imprint

Visit Tyndale online at tyndale.com.

Visit Tyndale Momentum online at tyndalemomentum.com.

Tyndale, Tyndale's quill logo, *Tyndale Momentum*, and the Tyndale Momentum logo are registered trademarks of Tyndale House Ministries. Tyndale Momentum is a nonfiction imprint of Tyndale House Publishers, Carol Stream, Illinois.

The Church Revitalization Checklist: A Hopeful and Practical Guide for Leading Your Congregation to a Brighter Tomorrow

Designed by Ron C. Kaufmann

All the examples and stories in this book are true. Names and some specific details have been modified to protect the privacy of the individuals involved.

For information about special discounts for bulk purchases, please contact Tyndale House Publishers at csresponse@tyndale.com, or call 1-855-277-9400.

Library of Congress Cataloging-in-Publication Data

A catalog record for this book is available from the Library of Congress.

ISBN 978-1-4964-5440-9

Printed in the United States of America

27	26	25	24	23	22	21
7	6	5	4	3	2	1

Dedicated to the memory of Ambrose Gilbert Sapp, a local church pastor who toiled in obscurity among the rolling fields of Kentucky, shepherding God's people in poverty without any glory or recognition. He faithfully preached the gospel until he died. May God grant us more like him.

Contents

Leading Your Church into an Era of Renewed Optimism

If God can save any *person*, he can save any *church*. The gospel embodies a movement—bringing people out of spiritual darkness and into eternal light. The gospel not only initiates a new life in us, it also sustains us throughout our earthly lives. Jesus saves each one of us in a moment of time. But he also supports us in every moment that follows.

What Jesus does for individuals, he also does for the church, the assembly of saved individuals. The Good News is both personal and corporate. If we believe any person is worth saving, we must also believe any church is worth saving.

Some local churches will die. But no church *should* die. Every congregation of God's people is worth the effort to revitalize.

Landon pastors a church in rural Iowa. When I asked him how God had called him to his congregation, he responded, "I was the only one who applied."

He knew that pastoring a small church out in the cornfields would be difficult. His friends all told him not to go. But God had a different plan, and Landon followed in obedience.

"I was twenty-seven years old, young and dumb. So I said, 'I'll take it.'"

Right from the start, he encountered turmoil and a lot of heartache. Between the time he was called and his first day on the job, about a dozen people left the church. Another dozen left after the first couple of Sundays. In a church of maybe six dozen total, losing a third of the congregation was a big blow. Forget the typical ministry honeymoon; that didn't happen. To Landon, it was obvious the church needed a culture shift and a quick change of direction.

Having grown up in the area, Landon grasped intuitively what he had to do. He went back to basics with a twofold strategy: building relationships and teaching biblical truth.

As he focused on preaching through entire books of the Bible and spent a lot of time in people's homes, this combination of truth and love started to turn the tide. But at the six-month mark, another round of church squabbles caused him to question the viability of his leadership.

"I was so discouraged, I wasn't sure I would make it."

But Landon stuck it out, and personal evangelism became the catalyst for change.

"I started working one-on-one, bringing people into the church myself."

The personal revival in his own soul gradually spread to the congregation. It took almost five years, but noticeable changes began to occur. Average attendance moved above one hundred for the first time in decades. They renovated the church campus and added an associate pastor. The children's ministry and student ministry began to thrive. As average Sunday attendance grew to more than 125, they added a second service. Most of the newcomers had no idea that this had been a struggling church of only a few dozen people not that long ago.

What made the difference?

"The pastors who stay are the ones who make a difference," Landon is quick to point out. "It's easy to say and hard to do. But every time I wanted to leave, there were no opportunities available. And every time an opportunity came my way, I realized I was in a place I didn't want to leave."

Landon doesn't consider himself thick-skinned or courageous. He believes that God gives strength through our willingness to persevere.

"It's not about how tough or brave you are. It's about endurance. You take your licks and keep going. And one other thing: Don't make major decisions when you're hurting."

The ups and downs of ministry are real. There's no way

3

to gloss them over or soften the blows. Landon has felt them all. But through his endurance, he saw God take a church from falling apart to falling in love.

"I love the people of this church deeply," Landon said. "They are my family."

In the end, the only pastor who applied for the position was exactly the one God wanted there.

Optimism Always Bends toward Hope

Though it may not *feel* like it from one day to the next, God has sovereignly placed you exactly where he wants you to be. Maybe you've been longing for a transition in your circumstances. Maybe you're ready to quit. Maybe you just got fired. Maybe your church has been in the doldrums for years, and you're losing hope that it could ever be any different.

Regardless of your circumstances, there are many things you can't control. But what you can always control is your attitude—your posture. As you persevere, I encourage you to bend toward hope. Most pastors have a sore back because they carry a heavy load. It hurts to bend toward optimism. When you lean into a better place, it won't be without pain. God will stretch you. But he also promises to fill you with hope, peace, and joy.

> I pray that God, the source of hope, will fill you completely with joy and peace because you trust in him. Then you will overflow with confident hope through the power of the Holy Spirit.[1]

To hear people talk, the church in North America is deteriorating.[2] Reading the reports of decline can be exhausting and discouraging. Some overstate how hard the church is falling, but few would deny that many local churches are not doing well. Perhaps *your* church is one of them. Maybe you're tired or disheartened. Maybe you're hurting. Don't give up. Your congregation is worth revitalizing.

Some churches reek of selfishness, but even the self-righteous and self-absorbed are worth redeeming. They just need help refocusing on serving others. God may be calling you to exhort a few saints. Be strong. Don't give up. Your church is worth revitalizing.

Some churches fight. A lot. Certain members, it seems, put on their cockfighting spurs for business meetings and dare the chickens to challenge them. Hostile churches need someone to set a good example—to show them how to fight *for* the church, not *with* the church. Be brave. Don't give up. Your church is worth revitalizing.

Some churches don't seem to have a clue when it comes to ministry, and people scoff at them. But Jesus never has—and never will—ridicule a church. The church is his bride. Every congregation deserves leaders who will lovingly shepherd them toward a greater purpose. Be resilient. Don't give up. Your church is worth revitalizing.

Some churches are immature—like a gangly middle schooler trying to impress the girls at skate night. The people seem more concerned about how they appear than who they are. Energy is poured into all the wrong things. If this is your church, you'll need to be the grown-up in the room. Middle schoolers don't mature well without guidance. Churches don't grow in discipleship without a mature shepherd. Be determined. Don't give up. Your church is worth revitalizing.

Revitalizing a church can be a lonely calling. It's hard work, but it's worth it. Your fellow pastors may wonder why you stick around. Your church may not understand at first what you're trying to do. But you're not alone. The Bridegroom is with you—always. He is committed to his bride. He has promised to build his church to overcome the gates of hell. Don't give up. Your church is worth revitalizing.

Psalm 22, one of King David's great prophetic psalms, contains a movement—from disorientation to orientation; from the anguish of feeling forsaken to a crescendo of praise and optimism. Confusion becomes clarity. Uncertainty transitions into certainty.

> My God, my God, why have you abandoned me?
>> Why are you so far away when I groan for help?
> Every day I call to you, my God, but you do not
>> answer.
>> Every night I lift my voice, but I find no relief. . . .
>
> Yet you brought me safely from my mother's womb
>> and led me to trust you at my mother's breast.
> I was thrust into your arms at my birth.
>> You have been my God from the moment I was
>> born. . . .

I will proclaim your name to my brothers and sisters.
    I will praise you among your assembled people.
Praise the LORD, all you who fear him! . . .

I will praise you in the great assembly.
    I will fulfill my vows in the presence of those who
        worship you.[3]

How does David get to a better place? Through praise. He praises God not only in times of blessing, but through the valleys as well. David's lament in Psalm 22 points to something greater. There is *purpose* to his disorientation, just as there was purpose in Christ's suffering on the cross.

In Psalm 22, Jesus is portrayed as a sacrificial lamb. But by Psalm 23, he has become the Good Shepherd. The green meadows he promises in Psalm 23 are possible because of his suffering in Psalm 22. The dust of death in Psalm 22 precedes the peaceful streams of Psalm 23.

Your disorientation has a purpose, so praise God through it. A people yet to be born need to hear a message of hope. Your praise today—even as you struggle—may be just the spark that ignites a gospel movement. Give God glory in the fog, through the disappointment, through the pain, through the valley of the shadow of death. There is a better place ahead.

Psalm 22 begins with God's silence, but silence does not mean absence. God is ever present, even when you don't perceive him. God will never neglect you or forsake you. He has you in his sights even when you feel completely lost.

7

David's psalm of disorientation is not about deliverance *from* death, but rather a deliverance *through* death. Jesus died so you can live. Jesus died so his *church* can live.

The movement of the gospel takes people to a better place. Bad news becomes good news. Death becomes life. This applies to you personally, and it applies to the church corporately. If God can save any person, he can save any church. Any church can live. Any church can *thrive*. Persevere. Lead your congregation to a better place.

The hinge of true hope is resurrection. Jesus defeated death. Through his resurrection, you can be optimistic about the future. Through his resurrection, you can have complete assurance in the present.

Resurrection hope conquers defeatism. You don't have to resign. You don't have to give up. With Jesus, your struggle is purposeful and powerful.

Resurrection hope conquers anxiety. Your concerns have answers.

Resurrection hope conquers fear. You can be calm in the storm.

Resurrection hope conquers doubt. God provides assurance even when you're not certain.

Resurrection hope conquers death. Your church isn't dead yet. Your church doesn't have to die.

Let's Do This!

In my congregation's tradition, we baptize by immersion. Some baptisms are more memorable than others. I'll never forget the young man who shouted, "Let's do this!" right before he was immersed. He was completely submitted to Christ, optimistic about God's mission, and ready to share the gospel. He came up out of the water to roaring applause. His optimism was contagious. The church shared his hope.

I don't wake up every morning saying, "Let's do this!" But I probably should. Every believer should. Biblical optimism is neither capricious nor superficial. It is a joy deeply rooted in hope. Biblical optimism is complete confidence that God has a plan and his plan will prevail.

Optimism always bends toward hope. Everyone hopes for something. In a general sense, hope is the feeling we get when we *think* that something we want is within our reach. This type of hope is not a certainty. It's just a feeling.

Hope rises. Hope falls. But what if we could hope for something that was truly within our reach? What if our collective hope led to collective praise? What if our hope led to something—or Someone—certain?

The Gospel of Luke records such a hope—a greater hope not determined in the finite realm of circumstances.

Some have called Luke's thesis "the Great Reversal." The last become first. The least become the greatest. The least of all sit at the table with the King. This is the hope suggested in the Old Testament book of Job, of all places: "At last the poor have hope, and the snapping jaws of the wicked are shut."[4]

Hope is a term often used in a context of doubt. When we say, "I hope my team wins," there is a hint of disbelief.

When we say, "I hope my church grows," you know it's not guaranteed. When I peer into the freezer and say, "I hope there is ice cream," the grim knowledge of my kids' appetites adds an element of doubt.

Biblical hope, on the other hand, conveys confidence and security. When the Bible uses the word *hope*, there is no inclination to doubt.

There's only one place to find certain hope. As the old hymn has it, "My hope is built on nothing less than Jesus' blood and righteousness."[5] This hope is certain. It's not just a feeling. This hope is collective. It's available to all. This hope is infinite and eternal. It never dies.

Cultural Christianity might be dead or dying. Maybe that's embarrassing for some. But I'm not embarrassed. We need more faith contenders and fewer church pretenders anyway. The Christianity I see in the New Testament is lean and determined. We're called to work out our faith while running a race. We're called to gird our loins with truth.

Church, let's do this! We can stand strong. We can exude joy. We can encourage hope. I'm optimistic about God's work. I'm hopeful about Christ's church in North America. You should be too.

The Other Side of Tomorrow

This book is more about what *should* happen than what *will* happen. The following chapters are more prescription than prediction. However, the book wasn't written in a sociological vacuum. The ideas here come from hundreds of personal interviews with pastors over the last six years through Church Answers and more than twenty years of research on the church.[6]

The primary method of exploration is qualitative, rather than quantitative. Qualitative research offers a richness and depth often missing in quantitative research. Qualitative methods account for complex social interactions in naturalistic settings.[7] The church as an institution will likely never be accused of oversimplicity. But at times, raw statistical data on the church, even if accurate, is too reductionistic. For instance, few doubt the decline of the church in terms of average weekly attendance. Six out of ten churches have either plateaued or declined in weekly attendance.[8] Many good researchers have acted as prophetic voices over the past several decades. The overarching narrative is true. The church, in general, is not well.

My desire is to focus more on the story than on the stats, though the quantitative facts are woven into the backdrop and cannot be ignored. At times, I'll bring them to the forefront. But when we dig into the particulars of individual stories, hope emerges. Just beneath the surface flows a spring of life. There are signs that a movement of God is afoot. The decline does not have to continue. Things on the other side of tomorrow might be better than we anticipate.

Almost all the research in this book occurred through interviews with pastors in smaller churches—or what pastor Mark Clifton points out are "normative size" churches.[9] The median church size in the United States is seventy-five people.[10] If you're under one hundred in average weekly attendance, your church is normal.

I realize that numbers do matter. Human curiosity always gravitates toward things that grow quickly. This attention can sometimes be negative, but it's not always wrong. At many large churches where Christ is proclaimed, God is saving scores of people.

The first megachurch in the US, the Moody Church in Chicago, helped make pastor D. L. Moody famous in the late nineteenth century. In the 1880s, the growth of the Metropolitan Tabernacle in London to more than five thousand in attendance drew some of the world's most powerful leaders to pastor Charles Spurgeon.[11] Big churches are still popular, and worship attendance growth remains a viable measure of success. And just as Moody and Spurgeon are heroes, not villains, we should not assume that today's megachurch pastors are antagonists in the continuing story of the church.

However, a subtle shift in the storyline has begun to develop. After five decades of exponential growth, the number of megachurches in the United States has remained relatively stable over the past ten years—somewhere around 1,600, or less than one percent of the estimated 350,000 churches in the United States.[12] More people attend these megachurches than ten years ago, mainly because of the multisite movement, but the total number of megachurches has remained surprisingly static. After a decade of this sideways trend, is it safe to claim that the megachurch movement is beginning to wane?

The next few years are crucial for the health of the North American church. Megachurches won't just disappear. People won't flock back into smaller churches just for a change of scenery. Though the megachurch movement has been more of a positive force for the gospel than a negative one, if the overall health of the church is to improve, I believe that a movement of non-megachurches must gain momentum.

I'm optimistic about tomorrow, but smaller and medium-size churches will have to move into a mode of exploration to take advantage of the opportunity. Adventurers do not embark with a spirit of pessimism. Sailors move into uncharted waters when they believe something better is just over the horizon.

I believe a blue ocean lies before us. This book is an attempt to chart at least one course into the unknown waters. It's exciting but also risky. My hope is to help pastors and church leaders see that the risk is worth the reward.

But even though I'm hopeful, I'm not a Pollyanna. A firm grip on reality is every bit as important to leadership as optimism and a can-do spirit. The trick is to get the right mix. We're not going to get it all right. Hope must be willing to sacrifice perfection for progress. Hope must also be willing to get up and move, even if we're unsure exactly where to go. Where *are* we going? Forward! Where is that? Right in front of us.

The primary focus of this book is on the near-term. We must start exploring *now*. Set your sights for five years from today, but hold the specifics loosely. If we've learned anything from the coronavirus pandemic, it's that the future can change on a dime. But God is unchanging. His faithfulness endures forever.[13]

Uncertainty forces us to abandon our self-reliance and surrender to the power of God. When we do, God is able to stretch our hope and build our faith. It's a hard lesson. It's a necessary lesson.

When faced with a *crux* moment, the temptation is to hit the pause button. But as we'll see in chapter 1, we should hit the reset button instead. We must come to grips with the reality that things will not be the same. And that's okay! A blue ocean awaits.[14] Something greater lies on the other side of tomorrow.

Leading Churches into a New Era of Optimism

Not all optimists are leaders, but every leader must be an optimist. As a leader in your church, you have a responsibility to convey a hopeful message to your congregation. Leaders take people to a better place. Pastors shepherd their congregations to a better place. Pessimism has no place in leadership— not even if you try to rebrand it as *realism*—and it will not move people to a healthier place. Pessimists are not leaders. Pessimists always see the worst case. Pessimists assume that evil will prevail over good. Pessimists—by God's design— cannot be effective pastors or church leaders, because the gospel by its very nature is optimistic.[15]

I've written this book primarily for church leaders. As a lead pastor who coaches other pastors, I view the church through the lens of leadership. My doctorate is in the field of leadership studies, and most of my writing and research is on church leadership.

I titled this introduction "Leading Your Church into an Era of Renewed Optimism" to draw a clear distinction between my outlook on the future of the church and the more somber tone of other recent books on the subject. *Pessimistic* may be too strong a word to describe those other works, but cheerful and optimistic do not immediately come to mind when you consider titles that include the words *autopsy, recession,* and *crisis,* for example.[16] My concern is that too much negativity might become a self-fulfilling prophecy, especially at the local church level.

Just because national trends point to a decline in the North American church does not mean *your* church must decline. Leaders cannot resign themselves to negative influences and outcomes. Your role as a leader is to translate the message of hope in your own context.

Don't deny the facts—of course not. Problem identification is central to any good revitalization plan, and it's important to recognize the current state of your church. But you and your congregation are not destined to continue on a path of negativity. In fact, your job as a leader is to compel people toward a new hope, a renewed optimism.

What if every church adopted the mindset of new hope? What if every church stood up and said, "We can do this!" What if we all encouraged each other with the truth that the gospel conquers evil and Jesus wins in the end?

The Kingdom of God knows nothing of pessimism. Pessimism in leadership leads ultimately to tyranny. I also believe that so-called *realism* on its own is too rigid. Realism detached from optimism can only describe a situation without prescribing a solution. Describing reality is the job of historians and journalists, not leaders. Historians look backward. Journalists report what's happening today. Leaders move people to the other side of tomorrow. And that requires optimism.[17] Optimism at its most basic simply means seeing that something *better* is *possible*. Optimism assures us that we don't have to stay stuck where we are. We can move, we can hope, we can take action.

My thesis is really quite simple: Moving your church toward the hope of tomorrow requires optimism. *The Church Revitalization Checklist* provides a way to implement this hope. Without a guide, it's easy to get lost. The checklist will keep you focused. God has sovereignly placed your church in a specific location for a reason. A better day is just on the other side of tomorrow. Optimism and hope will lead your church there.

All together now: *Let's do this!*

1

Hit the Reset Button, Not Pause

FAR TOO MANY CHURCHES hit the pause button when what they really need is a full reset. Depending on who's counting, somewhere between 65 and 90 percent of churches need some form of revitalization.[1]

Yes, there are times to pause, take a breath, and reevaluate, but some churches have been idling on the sidelines for decades. A lot of churches are still driving around in a 1982 Ford Escort—the bestselling car of the year with its 1.6-liter single-cam engine pulling a full 68 horsepower—and yelling "It still runs!" out the manually rolled-down window. Hitting the forty-year pause button is nothing to brag about. Just because it was popular way back when doesn't mean it should be driving your church today.

Here's a more compelling—and biblical—vision to drive today's church: "Anyone who believes in me will do the same works I have done, and even greater works, because I am going to be with the Father."[2]

Right now, your church has the opportunity of a lifetime. Sounds cliché, right? Except it's *true*. The promise Jesus made in John 14 should definitely get your attention.

The work Jesus did transformed people's lives. He taught. He healed. He saved. He fed. But that was only the beginning. Read that promise again, with some emphasis added: "Anyone who believes in me *will do the same works* I have done, *and even greater works*, because I am going to be with the Father."

We will do *even greater works*. Do you believe this promise? It's a hard one for me to grasp. Once you've resurrected someone from the dead, what "greater works" are even possible? I barely have the power to landscape a flower bed.

But what does Jesus mean by "greater"? Obviously, we don't have more power than the Son of God does. So how can our works be greater than his? I believe the word *greater* refers to geographical reach, not potency of power.

During his time on earth, Jesus was limited to three years of ministry in a small region of the world. After he ascended, and left the church to complete the mission, the amount of geography in play soon expanded to include North Africa, Asia Minor, and the southern reaches of Europe. And eventually the entire globe.

Notice the purpose of this expansion, in John 14:13: God's glory. Don't miss this: God promises us greater things through the church if we pursue his glory. The promise is that God will use us for greater things.

Ephesians 3:10 reveals the means of this promise:

> God's purpose in all this was to use the church
> to display his wisdom in its rich variety to all the
> unseen rulers and authorities in the heavenly places.

How will Christ be made known to the world? Through the local church. Through the extended geographic mission of the bride of Christ.

God will use you individually, and he will use the church corporately. The promise of John 14 is that he will use both in greater ways! You give God glory by believing in his promise that your church can change the community around you. Pessimism is anathema to God's calling for every local church. Optimism is required to lead a church forward in the work of the gospel.

Now is the time for a reset. If the COVID-19 lockdown taught us anything, it's that the church can adapt quickly to changing circumstances. When we were forced to shut the doors of our facilities, we had to completely rethink our approach. Churches everywhere made the move online, added outdoor services where possible, and looked for creative new ways to fulfill their mission. Physical distance became the norm for ministry, but churches found new ways to promote and preserve community.

Drive-in church became a thing again. What launched

Robert Schuller and the Crystal Cathedral in the 1950s was suddenly back in vogue.[3] Old-fashioned solutions paralleled new tech-based experiments. The team at my church covered the full spectrum, writing snail mail letters and making phone calls while also pushing the limits of the available technology to produce our weekly services. Some ideas worked better than others, but our church and others soon found their groove and started reshaping their methods of ministry.

The marriage of old and new technologies created a fresh new balance. Hitting the reset button doesn't mean we scrap everything we've been doing, but it does mean we're willing to try something new and experiment to see what works best.

The best art is often produced at a point of tension, such as when a crisis prompts an artist to think in new ways. The beauty that emerges from darkness and despair carries a particular power. Now is the time to experiment with new ideas. Recognize that the people of your church may be more willing than ever to accept creative new ideas. Not only have people become more accepting of innovation, but they are also more forgiving of fits and starts. Everything is different now, right? Or is it? Perhaps these kinds of opportunities have always been available. We just missed them as we puttered along with our church-as-usual programs.

Everything Is Different Now, Just like Always

The reset button is not a novel invention suddenly available to today's leaders. Over the past hundred years alone, dozens of *This changes everything!* moments have occurred.

For example, in 1966, Robert W. Taylor had an idea to create a nationwide computer network. Two years later, he wrote a white paper called "The Computer as a Communications Device," which became one of the founding documents of the internet.[4] Taylor was the director of the Pentagon's Advanced Research Projects Agency Information Processing Techniques Office—a long title later shortened to ARPAnet. What began with three terminals between the System Development Corporation in Santa Monica, UC Berkeley, and MIT would grow to dozens of networked sites by the early 1980s.

At first, the computer geeks did not want to share computing power across terminals. Why give up a share of your ability to process information? But when they came to realize the power of a dynamic medium over a static station, the entire world opened up. When my dad was in college in the 1970s, computer science was still dependent on physical punch cards. By the time I was in high school in the mid-1990s, my computer class was programming the school's first website.

To gauge the accelerated pace of change brought about by technological innovation, consider this: It took broadcast radio thirty-eight years to reach fifty million users. Television reached fifty million within thirteen years. The internet reached fifty million in four years—and changed everything.[5] But it wasn't the first time a pivotal event had changed the world.

The trenches of World War I obliterated the prevailing optimism of modernity—changing the face of warfare and international relations. With World War II, everything changed again. The Great Depression in the 1930s changed everything—as did the Great Recession in 2008 and 2009. The Long March and the ascendance of communism under Mao Zedong changed everything. So did the fall of the Berlin Wall. The mass production of penicillin in the 1940s changed everything. So did Rosa Parks and the civil rights movement. The creation of the state of Israel in 1948 changed everything. So did the terrorist attacks on 9/11. Albert Einstein, quantum physics, and the development of nuclear energy changed everything. So did space exploration, satellite technology, and mobile phones. Walt Disney changed everything. So did Nelson Mandela. The proliferation of credit cards changed everything. So did the housing crash and the bursting of the dot-com bubble. The emergence of HIV/AIDS in the 1980s changed everything. So did the coronavirus pandemic of 2020. "Everything is different now" has always been the case.

Every church has a reset button. Every pastor has an opportunity to press it. Don't wait for the world to change. The church is supposed to change the world. Stop lamenting our increasingly godless age. Let's build God's Kingdom.

Optimistic Responses to the Winds of Change

Here's a truth you can take to the bank: Change will be constant until Christ returns. Tomorrow will be different from today. Will tomorrow's differences be subtle or culture-shifting? It is impossible to predict.

During the coronavirus pandemic, many people learned

more than they wanted to know about logarithmic curves and regression analysis. Facebook became a statistics tutor as friends and neighbors began making predictions. But even the experts struggled with predicting what would happen next. We were living the truth of the old statistics adage: "All models are wrong, but some are useful."[6]

This chapter is less about getting an exact prediction right and more about getting the posture of leadership right. Get ready and start believing that God will do a great work. Bob Dylan's famous line "The answer is blowin' in the wind" is both truth and poetry.[7] We feel the wind, but we can't see it. We know it's there, but we can't grab it. The winds of change are all around us. No one can predict exactly what will happen on the other side of tomorrow. But we can prepare ourselves for an optimistic response. With 65 to 90 percent of churches needing some form of revitalization, something must be done. How did we get here? What answers might be blowin' in the wind? How can we respond optimistically?[8]

The Erosion of Evangelism

The first wind of change is a slowing conversion rate due to a decline of evangelism. Don't get me wrong: Some churches are growing. In fact, before the pandemic, about 30 percent were on a trajectory of increasing attendance and income.[9] Unfortunately, evangelism is not the driving force behind growth in many churches. Growth is more likely to come from *transfer growth* and *biological growth* than from evangelism or growth from conversions.[10]

Over the last few decades, a simple societal shift has occurred in the church. People moved from liberal churches to conservative churches and had more babies. The growth of conservative churches over liberal churches was first identified in the 1970s.[11] Liberal churches declined as congregants shifted toward more conservative churches. Additionally, conservatives have significantly more children than liberals—by a factor of 41 percent.[12] I am not making a qualitative judgment about theology or family size, but the facts are important to know. Facts are our friends.

Some churches are growing, but too few are doing the work of evangelism. The conversion rates of growing churches are almost the same as for any other church.[13] Evangelism programs were popular from the 1970s through the 1990s, but then churches began to cancel their evangelism programs and did not replace them with anything else. Though the efficacy of those programs was rightly questioned, the tragedy is that, rather than trying to develop more effective methods, churches just stopped trying to do evangelism training.

If you're a Christian, someone must have shared Jesus with you. Who invited you into the faith? Now it's your turn—and your responsibility—to share the good news of Jesus with others.

Most people don't share their faith for two reasons: *fear of failure* and *fear of rejection*. What if I don't share the gospel correctly? What if the person rejects the message? Or worse, rejects *me*! The problem with most evangelism efforts is that we plan more for failure than for success. But evangelism is one area where we should be the *most* optimistic.

God is not looking for the strongest, best looking, most eloquent, or most popular witnesses. He is looking for the most devoted.

You can hit the reset button on evangelism. Quite simply, it begins with you.

A few years ago, I sat with a group of eight elders who had hired me as a consultant because their church had noticed a decline in attendance. I asked for their annual figures. As I dove into forty years of data, a trend emerged. They had lost, on average, about eight people a year over a forty-year period. What was once a church of five hundred was now under two hundred.

"What do you think caused this decline?" I asked.

"Many of our members believe the new pastor is to blame."

"Really? He's in his twenties. Your problem began about fifteen years before he was born!"

"Your numbers must be wrong."

"These are the numbers you gave me!"

They wanted to make the problem more complicated than it was. When problems are complex, it's much easier to avoid responsibility and assign blame. But the problem here was obvious. They had stopped doing the work of evangelism.

So I said to them, "We have eight elders at the table here, and your church has averaged a loss of eight people per year. If you elders had simply done the work of evangelism yourselves, each of you winning one person to Christ per year, then your church would not have declined."

Optimism can be blunt. But the truth can also be liberating.

The return to an evangelistic outlook begins with leadership. Evangelistic churches have evangelistic pastors. Your church will respond if you *show* them evangelism in action rather than simply talking about it on Sunday morning. Set a personal goal of reaching one person for Christ every six months. Expand your outreach to include your staff and key leaders.

If you're hesitant, I understand. Salvation is God's work, not ours. At the same time, we cannot *fail* if we are *obedient*. What if the one thing holding back a large-scale revival is your disobedience? Be optimistic about evangelism—not for the sake of increasing your attendance numbers, but for the sake of changing your church's culture and promoting the growth of God's Kingdom. The healthiest churches inwardly are the ones most focused outwardly. If Jesus is the gravitational center of your life, you will naturally pull others toward him and into his body, the church.

A Larger Generation Gap

The second wind of change is a widening generation gap. Two major reasons exist for this widening gap: *technology* and *life expectancy*. Technological advances are increasing rapidly at the same time life expectancy is also increasing rapidly. Both are great trends. Both give us reasons to be optimistic.

People are living longer. People are advancing further. There are more years to enjoy and more things to do in those years. But with more years and more gadgets comes more tension.

"Open your Bibles. Turn on your Bibles. Roll out your scrolls."

That's the kind of language I now use when directing my congregation to God's Word. *Turn on your Bible?* That concept was completely unknown until recently.

The distribution of the Bible has always been aided by technological innovation. Papyrus sheets replaced leather scrolls. Parchment ultimately replaced papyrus. For a long time, only certain church leaders owned a Bible. In the 1300s, John Wycliffe—a revolutionary for his time—believed all Christians should read the entire Bible for themselves. He led a movement that translated the Bible into the language of the people. But until the mechanical, movable-type printing press was invented in the mid-1400s, few commoners had access to a Bible. Johannes Gutenberg's technological innovation enabled mass production of Bibles. Eventually, every family had a Bible. At some point, preachers started saying, "Turn to page 432." Now we open our Bible apps. Technology gives everyone access to every type of Bible translation for free.

I don't want to overplay the generational tensions with technology. There are Luddites of every age. However, many of our older brothers and sisters are witnessing rapid change in a way unimaginable during their youth. For my young children, rapid change is normal.

In 1900, only 25 percent of the US population had running water and less than 10 percent had a telephone. In 1900, no one had a refrigerator, radio, or washer and dryer. By 1965, Gordon Moore, the cofounder of Intel, predicted the doubling of electronic device capabilities every two years.[14] Today, some dystopian thinkers believe we will reach a technological singularity around 2050, in which machines become smarter than humans and take over the world. If Arnold Schwarzenegger is still alive then, we should all be afraid.

Not only are the rates of technological advances increasing, but people are also living longer, much longer than at any point in history. In 1900, a male infant was expected to live to forty-six, a female to forty-eight. By 2000, life expectancy of a male infant was seventy-four, and eighty for a female infant.[15]

What does this age trend mean for the church? Quite simply, the generation gap *feels* larger now because it *is*. People living longer means more generations than ever in the church. In 1900, most people died before the age of fifty. Therefore, church congregations spanned just two generations, with a smattering of older grandparents. Today, it's not uncommon to see four generations in a congregation. Today, large numbers of elderly congregants worship side by side with their great-grandchildren.

Church leaders now face the difficult challenge of unifying four—and sometimes five—generations. The preaching audience is as broad as it's ever been. Though I'm generalizing, most in the older generations expect lower use of technology in the church while those of the younger generations expect more technology. Just a few years ago, having your phone out in church was rude. Today it's encouraged—for giving, Scripture reading, and taking notes.

Church leaders deal with a greater variety of expectations from members as well, and those expectations change over time. For many in the older generations, the church is the one place where they can hang on to what's familiar. Technology introduces the unfamiliar. That feeling is not necessarily negative; it's simply a reality. The best church leaders will find ways to leverage technology in a way that is least disruptive for the older people while at the same time engaging for the younger people.

The tension inherent in a widening generation gap is both reality and an opportunity. As people live longer and technology continues to advance, generation gaps will continue to expand in our congregations. Just as we must embrace the increasing ethnic diversity in the United States, we must also embrace—not fear or try to ignore—the increasing generational diversity. In fact, the reset button exists because the older generations created it. After all, who invented all this new technology? The foundations for today's advances were laid decades ago.

I've been in pastoral ministry for more than fifteen years. I'm right at that age where the younger generations think I'm old but the older generations still think I'm young. This generational no-man's-land has taught me something. Many times, it's better to *show* people your vision rather than try to *explain* your vision. I've spent countless hours writing summaries for committees, creating spreadsheets for teams, and documenting history for business meetings only to meet a brick wall because people could not *visualize* the vision. One of the best ways to hit the reset button for all generations is simply to show them, rather than try to explain everything.

William is an example. He's a fortysomething worship pastor attempting to unify a multigenerational church. For years, he tried to explain to the younger generation why hymns are important. He spent countless hours trying to convince the older generation why a modern worship experience was necessary for the future health of the church. The people of the church were kind to William, but they didn't want to budge. Everyone feared the unknown.

Then one day he just did it. He *showed* them the new worship experience. The church loved it. In fact, people from both generations came up to him after a few weeks and said, "See, I told you so. We've been talking about this for years. I'm glad you finally started listening to us."[16]

If you're younger, please don't ignore the older generation. And if you're older, please don't fear the younger generation. The inevitable friction between generations can create beautiful congregations. But it will take all ages submitting to the Master, allowing him to mold and shape us together. Be optimistic. All creatures of our God and King can be a merry bunch of misfits. Safe churches don't change the world. You become an Acts 17:6 church by first being an

Acts 4:20 church. You will turn the world upside down when you can't stop speaking about Jesus.

Diversity Is Expected

What was once merely an ideal is now an expectation. Our churches must become more diverse. Hitting the reset button includes leveraging our ability to become more diverse.[17]

But is the United States *really* becoming more diverse? Many well-meaning people have asked me this question. If you live in an area that is still largely homogeneous, you may not see much ethnic diversity in your circles—at least not *yet*. But it's coming. The demographic landscape in the United States is reaching a tipping point and the Caucasian majority will soon become a minority.

My grandparents came of age when the US population was almost 90 percent white. My grandchildren will grow up in a nation that is majority nonwhite.[18] This shift can already be seen in preschools.[19] Ethnic diversity was once limited to large urban centers such as New York, San Francisco, Houston, and Miami. But diversity is now spreading everywhere—primarily among the younger generations.

In 1967, the US Supreme Court ruled that interracial marriage is legal. Since that ruling, in *Loving v. Virginia*, marriages between different races or ethnicities has increased more than fivefold.[20]

The issue of diversity is not only a demographic reality, it's a gospel reality. What humanity segregates, God brings back together. Racial segregation is a vile idea from the pit of hell.

If we genuinely believe the bride of Christ contains every tongue, tribe, and nation, then we shouldn't have a problem with marriages between tongues, tribes, and nations.

More importantly, our churches should reflect this demographic change. Indeed, the church should lead on the issue of diversity. Public schools will become ethnically diverse simply by who moves into the neighborhood. Why shouldn't our churches see similar patterns? As tribes and nations move in together, the church should reach out to enfold them. Ethnically diverse neighborhoods are not pre-Jonah Nineveh. They are a taste of heaven.

About fifty years ago, leaders in the church-growth movement started using the "homogeneous unit principle" to justify racial segregation. A homogeneous unit "is simply a section of society in which all the members have some characteristic in common."[21] It is based on the underlying assumption that "people like to become Christians without crossing racial, linguistic, or class barriers."[22] Even as they warned against ethnocentrism and racism, many of the movement's leaders favored a more segregated church.

The homogeneous unit principle evolved to become a rationale for churches not assimilating people across ethnicities. For example, proposals on how to deal with African Americans moving into white neighborhoods called for white churches to move out to the suburbs rather than work to become heterogeneous in the city. Calls to break the comfort of tradition in the church did not seem to extend to becoming *un*comfortable by reaching people of different backgrounds.

Now that our nation is reaching a demographic tipping point, these rationalizations from a prior generation are diminishing—as they should. The church must do the hard work of assimilating people of different ethnicities, generations, and socioeconomic backgrounds. The more diverse a church, the more it reflects the true gospel. An ethnically diverse church makes a loud statement for the transformational power of King Jesus.

We're getting better about embracing diversity, but we've still got a long way to go. The binary divide of white and black reached its apex in the 1960s. The nation has healed somewhat since then, but tensions still exist. In 2020, protests erupted following the murder of George Floyd in Minneapolis, at the hands of a white police officer. His last words, "I can't breathe," became a rallying cry for many who desired to see a greater focus on racial justice for the black community.

Studies have shown that most pastors believe in racial diversity, but it's still "more dream than reality."[23] About 85 percent of pastors believe in striving for diversity, but the vast majority do not shepherd heterogeneous congregations. Americans in general believe in diverse churches—about 78 percent believe churches should strive for diversity. However, only about half of Americans would be most comfortable in a multiethnic church.[24] Weekend worship services are still among the most segregated places in the United States. What can be done?

Though specific churches have sought to lead the way on diversity, a movement of hundreds or thousands of churches does not exist. Perhaps we're in the beginning stages of such a movement. I certainly hope so. I have a personal stake in this issue, as three of my children are white and one is black. But for a movement to pick up steam, a few things will likely need to occur:

1. Churches must pursue diversity on their staff. In most cases, churches will not become more diverse until leadership becomes more diverse. This diversity is especially important with the visible staff positions, such as pastors and worship leaders.

2. Heterogeneous mergers must become more common. Church mergers are becoming more prevalent. These mergers come in many shapes and sizes. However, we need to see more mergers between two (or more) congregations with different ethnicities. Most church mergers are homogeneous—two churches with a similar makeup of people. Stories such as the merger between Jacksonville, Florida's Shiloh Metropolitan Baptist Church (African American) and Ridgewood Baptist Church (white) are far too rare.[25]

3. Preschool and children's ministry must become more of a priority. Even if a church might resist a merger, or resist the idea of becoming multiethnic, the children of the church will never know the difference. If a church has a diverse preschool and children's ministry, it's more likely to become a multiethnic church within a generation.

Not only should churches pursue diversity organizationally, but every church leader can do something individually as well. In fact, it will take pastors and church leaders making the first strides to achieve cultural and racial diversity in our churches.

Start by developing individual relationships. You should intentionally develop a relationship with another church leader in your community who is not of your ethnic background. When you build bridges to other leaders in this way, you also tear down walls between congregations.

You can also begin new organizational relationships. You should get involved in an organization or event that is not part of your demographic group. Traveling to a different context—whether across the globe or in your own backyard—will broaden your worldview and enhance your understanding of cultural issues.

All pastors and church leaders should read more diversely. Read books, blogs, and publications that have a different ethnic audience than your own. Diving into the ideas of others strengthens your appreciation for their struggles and victories.

Listen to people of color. Perhaps the easiest way to grow as a multiethnic leader is to engage with and listen to other ethnic leaders. Simply pay attention to their social media feeds. Go to a meeting with them and observe. Attend their church and worship as they do. I bet you'll learn something.

The move toward racial and cultural diversity in our churches probably doesn't *feel* like a pressing need. The tyranny of the urgent seems to get our immediate attention. The need to grow in racial and ethnic diversity shows up more as a gnawing reminder that there is more to do. But this growth is important. In fact, the health of the church twenty years from now depends on our steps in this direction today. Be optimistic and take action. The gospel demands that we move in this direction.

Declining Attendance Frequency

Another wind of change affecting churches in the United States is a decline in attendance frequency. This applies to most churches, regardless of size or denominational affiliation.

It used to be that an active member was someone who came to church two or three times a week. Today, someone who comes to church twice a *month* is considered an active member.

Many reasons exist for this decline—from travel sports to the demise of cultural Christianity. Not every reason is bad. Some folks may be inching their way into church for the first time. Others may be returning to church after years of being gone. In most cases, however, people just fade away and don't attend as often.

On the surface, it may not seem so bad that a person misses one or two weeks out of four. But when a sizable portion of a congregation does not attend as frequently as they once did, it has a much more significant collective impact.

A simple exercise bears this out.

Church A has four hundred people who attend four out

of four Sundays. (Every pastor's dream, right?) Thus the church has four hundred members and averages four hundred in attendance.

Church B has four hundred people who attend three out of four Sundays. (Still not too bad.) But this attendance frequency means that the church averages three hundred in attendance each week.

Church C has four hundred people who attend, on average, two out of four weeks. (This pattern is probably more realistic in most churches today). Thus they average two hundred in attendance.

I'm sure you see where this is going. Each church has four hundred people who are part of the flock, but the average attendance at Church C is half that of Church A. Even without "losing" anyone, Church C is, for all practical purposes, half the size of Church A.

Here's the kicker: The true size of your church could be double the average weekly attendance, if not higher. As attendance frequency declines, the congregation will *feel* smaller even if it's actually getting larger. Many will wonder *Where is everyone?* on a Sunday morning, but the pastors and church leaders will *feel* the full ministry load. The people who attend less frequently still email, call, and set up counseling appointments. They still ask the pastors to do funerals and weddings and come to the hospital.

As people attend church less frequently, other symptoms begin to appear as well. For one, spiritual disciplines become weaker. As one discipline (attendance) goes by the boards, so do others. People who attend church less often are also likely to read their Bibles less, pray less, and share their faith less.

Communication becomes harder even as methods of communication improve. In a past era, the church used the Sunday morning gathering to communicate important information. Then bulletins became popular. Then churches started to utilize newsletters mailed to homes. Then they began using slides on a screen. Then email newsletters became prevalent. Now we have social media and texting services. At our church, we use no fewer than twenty pathways of communication. In an era of decreased attendance frequency, overcommunication becomes the norm to make sure we're reaching everyone.

As attendance frequency declines, so does congregational loyalty, and church hopping becomes even more common. Giving also becomes less consistent, though online giving and automatic deductions have helped to mitigate this problem. But the underlying reality remains: People who attend church sporadically tend to give sporadically.

As attendance frequency drops, swings in attendance patterns become greater as well. Three-day weekends can create greater dips. Holiday services can create greater peaks.

There is, however, an upside to the problem of declining attendance frequency. Since most churches are already experiencing the problem, solutions are likely to bring rapid gains. For example, if your church members attend, on average, two out of four weeks, and you are able to increase this pattern to three out of four weeks, your average attendance will increase by fifty percent. One of the biggest reasons for a church to decline is a drop in attendance frequency. And improving attendance frequency can be one of the biggest reasons why churches grow!

The Slow Fade of Denominations

In the past when a church wanted help, few lifelines were available. Denominations were the institutional foundation. Associations and districts provided a local support system.

Denominations, associations, districts, and networks still assist churches, especially smaller churches, but their ability to do so on a large scale is hampered by declining loyalty.[26] If denominations and local associations still had the ability to help in grand ways, many established churches would not be in decline. The lifelines still exist, but they are weaker today than in the past.

I worked with one church that sought help from their association, only to find that the resources were limited to a few workshops. Their denomination did not return phone calls because they were inundated with requests from struggling churches. When this congregation reached out to larger churches in the area for help, they found themselves in conversations about merging. They soon realized they would have to make their own way through a revitalization process.

The remnant of people in this church remembered the good old days of denominational and associational strength. They had supported each one faithfully for decades, only to find a crumbling shell when they themselves needed help.

The leaders of this church were shocked by how weak their association and denomination had become. They had been blind to the decline not only in their own church, but also in their denomination.

The old lifelines are long frayed and not likely to hold much longer. Most denominations are losing members and churches at a rapid rate. I believe denominations will continue to exist for the next few decades, but they will not be able to assist member churches the way they did in the past.

Some of the decline is due to the demise of cultural Christianity. Many people who once were nominally connected to a particular denomination are now completely detached—not only from the denomination but also from the local church. But the decline cannot be attributed solely to the exodus of nominally connected congregants. Even among those who are active in the faith, denominational loyalty is declining, especially among the younger generations. When a denomination is no longer in a growth mode, it eventually goes into survival mode. We should not celebrate this decline. The denomination as a Kingdom institution was a huge benefit to the mission of God.

Unfortunately, many of these institutions no longer provide the resources and financial backing needed to help revitalize struggling churches within their tribe. As denominations decline, funding goes down and the ability to promote collective interests begins to fade.[27] Denominations do not have the energy or funds to revitalize churches, mainly because the churches supporting the denominations are the ones in need of revitalization. It's a vicious cycle. The denomination can't help the churches because the churches can't fund the denomination.

There will always be individual cases of revitalization through denominational work, but a movement of revitalized churches is not likely to come from denominations. Revitalized churches will chart their own course, which is why I've written this book. I assume most churches will not receive large amounts of funding or resources from their denominations. The next chapter introduces the concept of a checklist, something that can be done by any church. The checklist includes seven points of emphasis that are essential to any revitalization process.

Maybe you feel like a lone voice crying in the wilderness. But like John the Baptist before Jesus, it may simply be that you are preparing the way. Keep moving forward. God just may send people into your wilderness who are ready for revitalization.

The Optimism of a Reset

When I hit the reset button on my Atari game system as a kid, it was often in a moment of frustration. I didn't like the outcome of a game, so I started over. Frustration may not be the best motive, but it can be channeled into a desire to do better. The church needs a reboot of evangelism. The church needs to address the widening generation gap. The church needs to meet the diversity challenge. And people need a reason to start attending church more often.

The reset button is a symbol for a new mindset—one that uses optimism to pursue revitalization in the church. As we will see in the next chapter, a strong comeback is possible.

2

The Revitalization Checklist

Complexity is the killer of church revitalization. But even the most streamlined and healthy organization has its layers of complexity. Any individual responsible for leading or managing seventy-five people (the median size of a church in the US) will tell you the job is full of complexities. Leading a small business with seventy-five employees is complex. Leading a school with seventy-five teachers is complex. Leading a nonprofit with seventy-five volunteers is complex. Leading a church is no exception.

One young pastor mentioned to me the struggle of managing twenty-six standing committees.

"How many people attend your church?"

"Four hundred."

They had a committee for every fifteen people in the church. The pastor was attending a meeting almost every night of the week to make the most basic of decisions.

Overstructured churches are complex by design, but even balanced or unstructured churches are not immune from the problems of complexity. Church leaders walk a precarious tightrope. Any given decision, comment, or observation—as well-meaning as it may be—can just as easily cause harm as bring healing.

A rural church in Indiana had a pastor-led model. For the most part, the congregation was happy for the pastor to make most of the decisions. The complexities arose not from the structure but from relationships within the church. Three of the more prominent families had a long-standing fight over some farmland. Apparently, adjoining property lines were an issue for three daughters who had inherited land from their father. At any given time, one of the families would stop attending. The pastor was often called upon to mediate disagreements.

Today we have access to more training and information than at any point in history. Ministry podcasts and books on church leadership are everywhere. Seminaries have moved online. The best preachers are available on demand on YouTube. Churches do not decline because training is unavailable; they decline because the leaders cannot implement what they already know. More information is not the answer. Neither is more skill or training. The solution is a simple system of accountability: a checklist.[1]

Why Use a Checklist?

I recently installed a blackboard in my office. New technology excites me, but there is something about the slow intentionality of writing with a piece of chalk. My blackboard has one purpose: It's where I organize my goals by the month in which they need to be accomplished. It's for my checklist. As the year progresses, I cross out completed tasks. The checklist has many uses, but three benefits are of critical importance: making my progress visual, providing constant accountability, and fostering a consistent focus.

Visual Progress

A manifesto is a written declaration of intentions. That's why I write my goals in a spot where I will see them on a regular basis. Start by finding a place that will work for you. A file on your phone or computer is not adequate. Our devices are already full of complexities and distractions. Select a place that's off-line and highly visible. For me, it's a giant blackboard in my office. My blackboard is the first thing I see when I walk into my office. The checklist will be of little value unless you use it to track visible progress.

Constant Accountability

Every morning, I follow a routine. I feed the dog. I make the bed. I make coffee. At times, I have forgotten to feed the dog. Even worse, I've made coffee and forgotten to bring it with me to the office. We can overlook the most basic of tasks. A checklist creates a system of accountability. Airplane pilots run through a checklist before every flight. Do they know how to fly the plane without it? Of course. But the checklist ensures that nothing critical is missed. The complexities of revitalizing a church often distract leaders from the most important tasks. Like the experienced pilot, you know how to get from point A to point B. The checklist is not a crutch for poor leaders. The checklist is a constant reminder for good leaders.

Consistent Focus

Too many pastors are swept into reactive mode by the inevitable fires that pop up during the week. The managerial side of pastoring can be frantic on any given day. With one phone call, the pace can switch from comfortable to chaotic. Most people understand and respect this aspect of ministry. What is less known is how fragmented daily activities can be. Much of pastoral management occurs in short conversations and activities—ten minutes here, fifteen minutes there. Quick hopscotch exchanges are normative in the daily management of the church. The visual checklist helps to keep you focused even as you react to the chaos. Some of the best pastors are crippled by spending most of their time being *reactive*. The checklist is a way to help you focus on being *proactive*. As noted in the previous chapter, complexities are everywhere in the revitalization process. But getting your church where you want it to be may be as simple as following a checklist.

Applying Your Checklist

Cake recipes have a checklist of ingredients and procedures. Space travel has a checklist called a launch sequence. Baking a cake is a relatively simple task. Sending someone into orbit is complicated. But both can be accomplished by following a process. But what about raising a child? What about revitalizing a church? Can a single checklist work for something so complex and variable? Each child is different. Each church is different. Checklists make sense for baking cakes and launching rockets. But they also are vital for tackling complex problems like revitalizing a church.[2]

Cultural, Not Comprehensive

The checklist I'm proposing is not a comprehensive list of everything you must do to revitalize your church. Such a list does not exist. A church turnaround starts with a rejuvenated *attitude* in the congregation, not an event that happens.[3] The revitalization checklist is a reminder of the goal—revamping your church's culture. The items on the checklist will keep you focused on the most important factors that will move your church forward—including culture-shaping questions to guide you through the inevitable complexities of the revitalization process.

Collaborative, Not Formulaic

You cannot lead a church revitalization on your own. The complexities are too much for one person to manage. In most churches, the complications are several years—if not decades—in the making. As a pastor or church leader, you may be the one guiding the revitalization process, but you cannot complete the checklist without the help of others.

Even the most knowledgeable and experienced pastor will find the complexities of church revitalization beyond the ability of any one person. The checklist is designed to encourage collaboration with other stakeholders and influencers in the church.

Flexible, Not Systematized

I am a firm believer in building good systems within the church. We have a system of communication in our church that includes newsletters, social media, texting, video announcements, and phone calls. But the checklist is not meant to replace those systems that are working well in a church. Just as you cannot build the world's greatest car by pulling together the best pieces from all the supercars and reassembling them, even the best church systems reapplied to your congregation may not work. The checklist is flexible enough to work within whatever systems or church polity you have. The goal of the revitalization checklist is not to dictate how to govern your church, or even how to systematize your church. The goal is to create a series of flexible checkpoints and questions to help move your church in a healthier direction.

Practical, Not Theological

Other good books provide a theological framework for church revitalization.[4] The checklist is meant to be a practical guide for church leaders. Right theology wrongly applied in church revitalization can do more harm than good. Conviction detached from empathy rarely produces lasting change in churches. Just because you know the right answers does not mean people will accept them. The purpose of this book is to help you connect your convictions to the hearts of the people who need to change.

The Language of Church Revitalization

Several terms are common when referring to church revitalization. Here is how I define them.

Church revitalization is the process of leading an established church to a place of better health, typically with an existing pastor and without changing the identity of the church.

An *established church* is a church with a defined location and history in a specific community.

Adoption is a newer term referring to the process of blending two congregations into one family. Some refer to this process as a church merger. I prefer the term *adoption* because it pulls in biblical language. Most adoptions occur when a larger, healthier church assimilates another church into a multisite system.

Fostering is a term connected to the adoption process in church revitalization. Fostering happens when a healthier church sends people and resources to help a struggling church over a set period of time, typically three months to a year.

Replanting occurs when new leadership enters an existing church and the church decides to be "a new church in the old building." Churches are replanted in several different ways: The building is given to a church plant; the building is shared with a church plant; or a core group decides to become a brand-new church with a replanting pastor.[5]

Relaunching is like replanting—with one key difference. A church relaunches by shutting down for a season and then reopening with a completely new identity.

A Typology of Church Revitalization

Because every church is different, every revitalization effort will have its own unique challenges. An urban church will use different approaches than a rural church. A church with a recent split is different from a church with a slow, decades-long decline. Though these differences will always exist, certain themes will emerge as you examine the broader scope of church revitalization.

In a simple Church Answers research project, we asked church revitalizers to categorize their work. From hundreds of pastor and lay leader responses, we were able to create a typology of church revitalization. The figures below represent the percentages of churches we found in each category.[6]

- *Geriatric churches* (40 percent): The median age of the church's members has increased significantly over the past several years. Few, if any, children or young families are present.
- *Great Omission churches* (25 percent): The church's ministries, resources, and efforts are focused inward

with hardly any evangelistic efforts. People either give lip service to outreach or simply stop caring about the lost.

- *Ex-neighborhood churches* (15 percent): The membership of the church does not reflect the demographics of the community. The church is a cultural island in the neighborhood. Typically, few people from the immediate community attend the church. Most members drive in from other communities.
- *War-torn churches* (12 percent): These churches have a reputation for fighting, conflict, harsh treatment of pastors, and—often—schisms and splits. There is a palpable tension at meetings and even in casual conversations around the church. The leaders pour most of their energy into mediating disputes and responding to arguments.
- *Mismatched leadership churches* (8 percent): The pastor is not the right leader for moving the church forward. In many cases, the pastor has no love for the community and may demean the people who live there. This leadership mismatch is often the product of an older pastor hanging on too long and not having a vision for the future. A younger pastor with overly idealistic desires for the church can also be a poor fit for effective change.

Though estimates vary, several thousand churches close their doors every year.[7] These categories represent some of the reasons why churches decline to the point of death. Maybe your church has symptoms that look like one or more of these categories. Don't despair. There is hope! The next several chapters present a positive perspective on how your church can make a comeback.

Seven Points of Church Revitalization

The next seven chapters will flesh out the church revitalization checklist and provide practical guidelines for leading cultural change in your congregation. The checklist is not comprehensive, but it's a quick way to remember the most important aspects of church revitalization. Put these checkpoints on every staff agenda. Write them on a whiteboard or blackboard in your office. Carry them into every committee meeting. Each part of the checklist contains a question intended to cut through the complexity of church and ministry management and focus on what is essential for positive change.

- **Priorities:** How do you discern what is most urgent?
- **Pace:** How fast can you lead change?
- **Perspective:** Are the church's expectations properly aligned?
- **People:** What is your true capacity to move forward?
- **Place:** Is your church facility ready for revitalization?
- **Purpose:** What can you do to shift your church to an outward focus?
- **Pathway:** What is the most realistic next step?

After years of research with thousands of churches, these seven checkpoints have emerged as fundamental to the revitalization process. Your church can move forward. The other side of tomorrow is looking good. Get excited. Be optimistic. Begin to notice the work of the Holy Spirit. God wants every church to be revitalized—including yours.

3

Priorities

Tending to What Is Most Urgent

CHURCHES ARE SIMULTANEOUSLY fragile and resilient. Every Sunday can feel like the precipice of disaster, a matter of moments before everything collapses into the garbage fire of Gehenna. Yet the same church survives year after year, decade after decade. Struggling churches tend to maintain constant tension between fragility and resiliency. It's the perpetual state of not quite dying.

This feeling of suspended animation creates a climate in which church members learn to survive but never thrive. The organizational culture has just enough momentum and life to get to the next Sunday, the next month, the next year. So many churches seem to be hanging on by their fingernails, but those fingernails prove to be incredibly strong.

After years of relative dormancy, any progress feels monumental. This was certainly the case at my first church. I was twenty-four years old, had no experience as a preacher, and lived two hours away from the facility. My girlfriend at the time (now my wife) noticed a pull-tab advertisement for a preacher on a bulletin board at her college. None of the tabs had been pulled. I had recently mentioned to her my calling to preach. She knew it was the right church for me. When I called the number, the person on the other end of the line asked when I wanted to start the service on Sunday. I thought it was an odd question. Later I learned they had not held services in about two years.

On my first Sunday, six people came to worship. It was late summer in Kentucky. There was no air conditioning. I was surprised they expected me to preach the sermon *and* lead the songs. The piano was out of tune, so I led hymns using a karaoke machine. The church was barely alive, but the people were energized and excited. They had thought no one wanted to be their pastor. I didn't know any better. God took two negatives and made a positive.

This was in 2004, when the idea of relaunching or restarting a church didn't exist. Church revitalization as we know it today was a concept in its infancy. I was there because no other church would consider me. They accepted me because they had no other choice. We started with a simple canvassing project, going door-to-door in the community and asking two questions: Do you know Jesus? Do you want to donate money to help the church?

God gave us opportunities to share about Jesus, and he gave us enough funds to install air conditioning. The community started talking about the old church that had new life. It had been founded in 1856, the building dated to 1924, and the rural community didn't want to lose the history that the church represented. Our efforts to revitalize the church became a symbol of a greater desire to revive a struggling community.

One of the first questions I asked of the lone deacon was, "What's the deal with the old bell out front?"

"I don't know, but it's really important."

On our first work day, the deacon handed me a paint brush and gave me the honor of painting the bell red. Why red? I don't know, perhaps it was the only color of paint the church had on hand.

Everyone in the community loved the red bell. We didn't know the history of the bell. We didn't intend for the red color to mean anything. But when it rang every Sunday morning, people in the tiny, rural community knew what it meant.

Before the red bell, most people referenced our historic graveyard. That was the wrong symbol. After we painted the bell red, it was the lively ringing every Sunday that people discussed. The church began to gain some momentum, but I was too young, had no experience, and was leading completely from ignorance. Only by God's grace did we survive.

It turned out our strategy worked—going door-to-door and telling people about the gospel while asking for money. Though I certainly don't recommend church revitalization by the seat of your pants, God used our genuine desire to save a dying church.

My goal in this chapter is to help you answer a key question: *How do I discern what is most urgent?* As you work through the checklist, start by diagnosing the problem.

Discerning the Drivers of Decline

The tiny, older congregation meeting in a derelict church building is a common image when introducing the topic of church revitalization. Indeed, there are many churches that fit the bill. The decline is obvious, especially if the church used to be several times larger decades ago. Many of these churches were once thriving, only to go through a long season of slow deterioration. What caused the downturn? How did it begin?

Churches decline for two main reasons—both having to do with a shift in priorities. First, they lose passion for the Great Commission and the Great Commandment. Second, as a result, they no longer give God glory. When a church no longer pushes outward with the gospel, the people will no longer look upward to God's glory. A church lacking both an outward and upward perspective will inevitably move in the other two directions: *inward* and *downward*. Inward churches always decline.

Misaligned priorities happen over time, and they pile up

on each other. In this section, take note of how many misaligned priorities characterize your church. Rate each one by how often the problem occurs, and then add up your score.

1. *Nostalgia is more prevalent than devotion.* The church's history is discussed more than the Bible. The past is the hero, not Jesus. People are more upset when something is out of place in the heritage room than they are with knowing their neighbors are lost. Memories of the past bring more emotion than the mission of the present.

Never	Rarely	Sometimes	Often	Always
1	2	3	4	5

2. *Polity is an end, not a means.* People refer to the bylaws as if they should never change. In this environment, the government of the church dictates how the church ministers. Business meetings are often rancorous, and parliamentary procedures are used as leverage rather than a simple means of conducting business. Loyalty to the denomination is more important than how loyal the people are to each other. Pastoral tenures are short.

Never	Rarely	Sometimes	Often	Always
1	2	3	4	5

3. *Traditions detach the church from community culture.* The church rebels against looking like the community. In the worst cases, the church grows to resent

the community rather than loving the neighborhood. These churches hang on to traditions that hinder the work of the gospel.

Never	Rarely	Sometimes	Often	Always
1	2	3	4	5

4. *Debt becomes a drain on resources.* There are good uses of borrowing. Sometimes a needed capital project would not happen without a modest level of debt. But if more than 20 percent of the budget is used for debt service, cash flow can become an issue. Debt-heavy churches often must defer facility maintenance in order to pay the bank.

Never	Rarely	Sometimes	Often	Always
1	2	3	4	5

5. *Preferences override God's mission for the church.* Internal hostility over preferences put people at odds with each other. Rather than fighting a battle against the spiritual forces of darkness, the church becomes a battleground for pet programs, favorite songs, styles of worship, and approaches to ministry.

Never	Rarely	Sometimes	Often	Always
1	2	3	4	5

6. *Generational power struggles exist.* The older generation clings to power. The younger generation refuses to accept responsibility. Families are split as some leave

for other churches. The church struggles to find multi-generational teams of volunteers. The older generation comes to one service while the younger generation attends another.

Never	Rarely	Sometimes	Often	Always
1	2	3	4	5

7. *The church becomes a platform for leaders.* Success is more important than accountability. In extreme cases, the power structure hides sin issues among the leaders. Leaders care more about their own reputation than serving the church. They use the church to further their own endeavors in the community.

Never	Rarely	Sometimes	Often	Always
1	2	3	4	5

8. *Comfort with the status quo outweighs a willingness to sacrifice.* In this environment, apathy becomes a contaminant polluting the mission of the church. Status quo churches act more like social clubs than Kingdom outposts. Groups in the church are less about Bible study and prayer and more about friendship cliques in which outsiders are not welcome.

Never	Rarely	Sometimes	Often	Always
1	2	3	4	5

9. *The people have an unhealthy fixation on the church's facilities.* The congregation cares more about the building

than they do about people in the community. For many, the building *is* the church. In severe cases, the church campus becomes an idol. More time is spent discussing the building than anything else.

Never	Rarely	Sometimes	Often	Always
1	2	3	4	5

Now total your score.

9–15: Churches in this range have an extraordinarily healthy understanding of priorities.

16–21: Churches in this range are healthy, but some emerging symptoms of misaligned priorities are evident.

22–27: Misaligned priorities are causing some decline. Without intervention, scores in this range represent a tipping point toward a decline in the health of the church.

28–33: Misaligned priorities are causing disunity. Few churches in this category show any sign of an outward focus.

34–45: Churches in this range are unhealthy and wayward. They have lost their sense of doing God's mission for God's glory.

The next section demonstrates how churches can begin to realign their priorities and regain a proper sense of urgency.

Recovering a Sense of Urgency with the Right Priorities

Leading a church into a new era of optimism means using every possible strength of the congregation. Churches are unique, but some common themes of healthier congregations will emerge as you build a sense of urgency with the right priorities.

Focus More on "Going Out" Than "Growing Big"

The desire for growth is what drove many churches to create programs of evangelism in the latter half of the twentieth century. Numerical increases became the goal during the church growth movement.[1] As the programmatic culture faded, churches canceled these evangelism efforts without replacing them with better alternatives. Perhaps "grow big" was not the greatest of motives, but at least churches were doing something to propagate the gospel.

Churches that grow stronger in the next five years will be focused on a "going out" effort. The strength will be in a twofold strategy. First, the church's culture will favor moving into the community. Second, the leadership will train the congregation to be ready for evangelism opportunities—thus fulfilling "their responsibility . . . to equip God's people to do his work and build up the church, the body of Christ."[2]

A healthy outward movement is driven more by obedience

than by seeking numerical growth. Serving the community can take various forms—from opening up church facilities during the week as a place for community groups to gather, to helping the local homeless shelter, to creating a food bank, to developing a school of performing arts. But serving alone is not enough. Pastors and church leaders must equip the congregation to vocalize the gospel as they serve. Unfortunately, far too few churches have harnessed the power of combining a culture of service with a willingness to share the gospel. A healthy church has an acute concern for the collective needs of the community while at the same time maintaining a desperate heart for the lost individuals in that community.

Embrace Children, Don't Just Tolerate Them

There are two kinds of churches: those that embrace children, and those that tolerate them.[3] Most churches are not rude toward kids, and I've never seen a church sign stating "No Kids Allowed." However, families that visit your church will know whether you embrace their kids or not. Churches that welcome children have a higher likelihood of retaining their families.

Here's a reality that has come into focus as church congregations age: Your church will not grow larger with the oldest generation. Older members provide stability, wisdom, and important resources, but for churches to grow and remain healthy, they must reach, enfold, and retain the younger generations. No church should neglect the care of its older generations. At the same time, they must focus their outreach strategies on the younger generations. This is one of the natural tensions that will only increase as the church becomes more multigenerational.

Embracing the children means understanding that messy is normal and natural—even healthy. Children have not yet mastered the godliness of cleanliness. They can turn the snack table in a Sunday school room into a work of abstract impressionist art. Children who are learning to take in God's Word, learning to worship, and learning to love Jesus are going to be messy. The line of smudges on the wall about two feet high is there because little hands are dragging as kids walk the halls. Messy is simply part of embracing the children in your church.

Embracing children means valuing noise over perfection. Children make noise in worship. Children make noise in classes. Children make noise in the parking lot. They cry. They laugh too loud. They scream and yell. Some churches try to suppress the noise. Other churches tolerate it. The most successful, healthy churches value the noise. I've heard of churches that don't allow children below a certain age in the worship service. Try to bring an infant into the worship space, and they'll stop you like an irate Pharisee with a bad case of the Mondays.

Embracing children means protecting them at all costs. Child security is a discipleship issue—and one of the most important. If you believe in the Great Commission, you will create robust security measures for children. Jesus says, "I am with you always."[4] A low-security church teaches children "I am with you sometimes."

Embracing children means investing in children's ministry. Is your children's pastor the lowest paid ministry team member? Does your children's budget match your worship budget? A church that embraces children will invest in ministries that support children. A church that merely tolerates children will give them the monetary leftovers. If it is easier to cut your children's budget than your technology budget, you most likely are not embracing children in your church.

Embracing children means understanding church at their level. A lot of churches seek out the perspective of parents—and you should! Helping parents create God-centered homes rather than child-centered homes is one of the core elements of family discipleship. However, you should not neglect the children's perspective. Ask them about their experiences, their feelings, and their opinions. When you understand church at the level of a child, you are better positioned to guide children toward Christ.

In Luke 18:15-17, Jesus invites the children to come near. In Mark 10:13-16, he embraces the children. Churches that welcome and embrace children are like Jesus. In fact, Jesus becomes angry at the disciples for discounting the value of children. The next time a child cries out in church, don't get angry at the child. Get angry at the person who is angry at the child. Children are a blessing from God and churches should make them a priority. On the other side of tomorrow, a stronger church will embrace children, not just tolerate them.

Let New Believers Disturb the Peace

Optimistic churches emphasize evangelism and embrace children. They also expect new believers to be disruptive catalysts. Healthy churches are always messy. As God blesses a church with many new believers and increasing numbers of children, the life of the church is bound to become more chaotic, not less. When your church is moving in the right direction, it's going to feel messy.

I remember baptizing a young woman who accepted Christ shortly after getting out of prison. While we were in the baptistry area, the worship pastor said to the congregation, "Everyone knows this song! It's a classic!"

As the people sang a familiar hymn, I turned to the woman and asked, "Do you know this song?"

"I've never heard it in my life."

"That's okay. You'll have plenty of opportunities to learn it."

I'll never forget explaining the Lord's Supper to a new believer.

"What's with the plastic cups and sips of grape juice?"

Or the time someone pointed out an odd decorating fad.

"Why do churches have fake plants everywhere? It's so strange."

Or how often we call each other funny names.

"Is everyone here related? What's all this brother and sister stuff?"

The church is moving in a healthy direction when new believers are disrupting the peace. Their questions and comments will cause you to rethink many things. Spend the next five years focusing on three key areas: evangelism, children, and new believer assimilation. Your church may not increase in size dramatically during the five years, but it will grow in many healthy ways.

Celebrate the Right Victories

You become what you celebrate. In most cases, the culture in an organization will follow whatever the leaders decide to champion. The same applies to churches and pastors. If you celebrate a past era, the culture of the church will reflect that past era. If you celebrate people coming to Christ, then the church is likely to value evangelism. If you celebrate new members and assimilation, the church is likely to value hospitality. If you celebrate numbers, then the church culture will desire numerical growth.

When I asked one pastor the secret to the turnaround in his church, he smiled and said, "We celebrate the victories."

Baptisms and birthdays are common celebrations at Sawgrass Church in rural central Florida. Baptisms, of course, are celebrations of people accepting Christ. The birthday celebrations include a time in which the children are taught about spiritual birth through salvation. They eat cake and hear the gospel. These celebrations are common now, but it was not always the case. When Pastor Don arrived at Sawgrass, the church had dwindled to a few dozen people after a difficult split.

Don came to the pastorate later in life. He began in his

forties and served about eight years on staff at another church. Then his mentoring pastor gave him an opportunity he couldn't refuse: "I want to put you in a spiritual wasteland."

The community around Sawgrass Church was rural and poor. The church was hurting and without direction. In fact, the one person who voted against Don becoming the pastor said the reason was "we can't pay him." But Don didn't see hopelessness. He saw opportunity and something to celebrate.

He went to work quickly, developing an emphasis on evangelism and discipleship. Worship improved. He sharpened his skills as a preacher. More than anything, Sawgrass Church celebrated people getting saved and baptized. Drawn by the celebrations, people started drifting back into the church. Families started coming.

Over the next three years, the church took off. Attendance grew to 125 on average. Then it spiked to almost two hundred. Don launched a second service. Without any money set aside in the budget, the church found a way to pay for $200,000 worth of renovations—all cash, no debt.

Eight years later, the church is still celebrating. Recently, they had a big party for baptism number 150.

Why has God provided such success? Don gives a simple answer: "We pray for softballs—people ready to receive Christ. God sends them to us and we are ready to share Jesus."

Celebration is such a central piece of the Sawgrass culture that they do it at every service. Every Sunday morning and evening service has a meal. Same thing on Wednesday nights. And they also take meals into the community.

"We are a church that eats!" Don says.

Recently, the church began to share the celebration model with other churches, helping two congregations in their community with a revitalization plan. They are also planting a church in a coastal area of southwest Florida.

What was once a spiritual wasteland is now ground zero for a gospel celebration. An optimistic leader will celebrate what he or she wants the organization to become. Start celebrating what you want to become and watch the culture change.

Outward + Upward = Onward

Two movements—outward and upward—should determine every priority in the church. All churches are called to reach outward. All churches are called to love their neighbors. All churches are called to reach the nations. Outward movement into the neighborhoods and to the nations will naturally create another movement—an upward movement to give God the glory. The only way to move forward is to set a priority on the outward movement of the Great Commission coupled with the upward movement of praising God.

Outward + Upward = Onward.

As you work through the first part of the checklist, use this formula for every priority in your church. How can you discern what is most urgent? Whatever moves your church outward and upward will also propel you onward.

4

Pace

How Fast Can the Church Move?

I'll never forget my first week as a full-time pastor. Books were unpacked. Sermons and lessons were written. Then I called my dad, who had served as a pastor for several years.

"What should I do now?"

"Give it another week. You'll get busy."

He was right. The deluge of phone calls and meetings started after my first official Sunday. My time as a bi-vocational pastor helped prepare me, but I was now shepherding ten times the number of people. I had not even started, and already the pace felt like a sprint.

It's one thing to know *what* to do. It's another thing to know *how fast* you can do it. Leading a church revitalization with a hopeful tone is a delicate balance between patience and urgency. You must have the patience to walk with people and the urgency to encourage them to pick up the pace.

"It's my first week, what should I change here?"

Perhaps new pastors don't vocalize the question, but I know they think it. At least, I don't believe I'm the only one who thinks that way. The default setting to change something is only natural for a good leader. Having a vision means being dissatisfied with the status quo.

In my book *Obstacles in the Established Church*, I dedicate an entire chapter to change management. A dedicated chapter is necessary here as well. Leading change is one of the greatest pain points in ministry. The honeymoon period for many a new pastor has ended because of the first real change effort. Resistance to change is one of the largest hurdles in leadership. I once had a handful of pencils launched at me when my tweaks to a church potluck were discovered. I learned not to mess with potlucks. Luckily, the pencils weren't that sharp.

How fast can I lead change? The answer to this question is critical for any church revitalization effort. The second point on the checklist involves assessing your congregation's pace of acceptance.

The Pace Acceptance Matrix

You may know the right thing to do. Getting others to accept and implement the right thing is what separates leaders from dreamers. As you consider the pace of change, use the matrix below to help you identify areas of potential resistance. All change involves people. Therefore, start by assessing the people in your congregation when considering the pace of change.

HOW RESISTANT TO CHANGE?	*Those older than you*	*Those younger than you*
Those before you	High resistance	Some resistance
Those after you	Some resistance	Low resistance

The matrix identifies four groups of people. Everyone in your church will fit into one of these four groups. Granted, this matrix oversimplifies individual nuances, but it is a helpful starting point when determining the potential resistance to change in your congregation.

Those Before You and Older than You

This group was part of the church before you arrived, and they are older than you as well. The longer your tenure, the smaller this group becomes—as you get older and new people come to the church. This group will be at its peak on your first day, and there is a strong likelihood they will be highly resistant to change, especially fast-paced change. But if you can gain their support, they are also the group most likely to champion and sustain change.

If you are a new pastor, many in this group may be silent for a season, waiting to see what kind of changes you implement. If you are a long-tenured pastor, you already know this group well. Somewhere between years three and five, this group will either start supporting you, elevating their concerns, or exiting quietly.

Those After You and Older than You

If you are a younger pastor, this group has the potential to be large and growing. I started pastoring at age twenty-four. For a decade, most people who joined the church fit this category. People join a church for a variety of reasons, but for the group that comes after you, you can at least be assured that they did not rule out your church because of you. Most will naturally show you some level of support from the beginning. But that doesn't mean they won't show some resistance to change. It depends on their prior experiences. The *pace* of change will not be as much of an issue for these people as the *type* of change. Too many changes that shift the culture of the church away from what they thought they were joining can create some resistance.

Those Before You and Younger than You

One of the surprises for new pastors is how some in the younger generations—particularly those who grew up in the church—can be just as resistant to change as those in the older generations. Younger folks tend to be more tolerant of fast-paced change, but if the change touches lifelong, generational connections, it can create resistance. Don't assume that all the young people will embrace your proposed changes simply because they're young. If you are older than forty, you likely already know this principle intuitively. Parents who are raising children in the church often have set ideas like the older generations. Millennials with children are settling into patterns and programs just like their grandparents did decades ago.

Those After You and Younger than You

The group least likely to resist change are those who joined the church after you and are younger than you. But *low* resistance to change does not mean *no* resistance. Even this group has a pushback point. Constant change efforts, especially a string of unsuccessful attempts, will cause anyone to challenge their leaders. This group, however, will generally accept a greater pace of change than the other three groups.

Gauging Pace Acceptance

People are complex. Resistance to the pace of change is common. Even the most banal changes can drum up opposition. Some college football programs have found that the smallest tweaks to the team's uniform can cause controversy. Who knew shades of green, blue, or red would rile up otherwise sane adults? The same kind of resistance occurs in the church.

What kind of opposition can you generally expect? How accepting of change will your church be? The following exercise will give you some insight into the potential for resistance in your congregation. In each of the matrix squares, estimate the percentage of your congregation that falls into each category. Your church database may be able to produce exact numbers. If not, then estimating these figures will work for the sake of the exercise. After making your estimates, compare your results to the examples below to determine whether your church is likely to be *high* resistance, *mid* resistance, or *low* resistance.

High-Resistance Churches

In churches with a high resistance to change, often more than half the people will be older than the pastor and less than half will have been at the church longer than the pastor. The percentage mix of this church can mean that change will be slow because the power structure of the church will not have it another way.

HOW RESISTANT TO CHANGE?	Those older than you	Those younger than you
Those before you	50 percent	20 percent
Those after you	20 percent	10 percent

Mid-Resistance Churches

Churches with a mid-level resistance to change often have an even mix of older and younger, longtime and new members. These churches can handle an increased pace of change, but it comes at a cost. The even split between new members and longtime members eventually leads to tension between the two groups as the power structure shifts within the congregation.[1]

HOW RESISTANT TO CHANGE?	Those older than you	Those younger than you
Those before you	25 percent	25 percent
Those after you	25 percent	25 percent

Low-Resistance Churches

A church with a younger and newer mix of people tends to be more accepting of a faster pace of change. As mentioned previously, a low resistance to change does not mean no resistance to change. But when more than half the people are younger than the pastor and more than half are newer to the church than the pastor, the pace of acceptance goes up considerably.

HOW RESISTANT TO CHANGE?	Those older than you	Those younger than you
Those before you	10 percent	20 percent
Those after you	20 percent	50 percent

Deciphering the Best Pace of Change

Every church must change. The issue is how quickly. Let's assume someone needs ten surgeries to treat a particular problem. The doctors know what to do. The diagnosis and prognosis are clear. Then the patient speaks up.

"Doc, I'm ready. Do all ten surgeries at once. I understand it won't be easy, but I want to get it over with."

Even though the patient says he or she is ready, no doctor would attempt ten surgeries at once.

Likewise, your church may say they are ready for change, but they can only handle so much at a time. Just as the human body cannot cope with multiple procedures at the same time, a church can only handle a certain amount of change at a certain pace. Trying to do too much puts the body (physical or corporate) in jeopardy of failure.

Not every change can be implemented gradually. When there's a fire, someone must break the glass and douse the flames with the extinguisher. Quick changes can make messes. But not every change requires a fire marshal. Many changes can occur gradually or in phases. When gradual change is possible, one of the worst things you can do is "create a fire" to expedite the change. Fires can get out of hand, and they are always destructive. Additionally, most people don't like to follow a leader who is an arsonist.

Even when people in the church explicitly state they are ready for change, too much change too quickly is a shock to the system. Even if people think they're ready for the shock, it still hurts. And then the leader wonders why they shouted.

"You said you were ready!"

"But that hurt!"

It happens all the time.

If you're a leader and you have sufficient time to make a change, take your time. Unfold your map, plot your course, and enjoy the journey.

The Case for Gradualism

The power of focusing on one thing is that it starts to build momentum. Focus on one key change for six months, then add another change and shift your focus there for the following six months. Struggling churches stop struggling and start making progress when they refocus their survival energy into a series of one-thing next steps. Over the course of two years, one success becomes four. Far too often, pastors want to operate on all the sick areas of the church at once. No surgeon would attempt multiple procedures at the same time. Neither should pastors.

Most organizations are too complex for one person to lead a change effort alone. Any organization of seventy-five people—the median church size in America—is a complex system of relationships, opinions, maturity (or immaturity), and attitudes. You alone are not going to be the cause and effect at your church.

Momentum builds with each incremental step of change. Optimists are willing to stick to a reasonable pace. The concept of a flywheel is helpful. Jim Collins brings this picture to light in his book *Good to Great*. He describes "a massive metal disk mounted horizontally on an axle . . . and weighing about 5,000 pounds. Now imagine that your task is to get the flywheel rotating . . . as fast and long as possible."[2]

Your first efforts produce imperceptible movement, but you keep pushing. A few others join you, and the flywheel moves slightly faster. Push after push, momentum gradually builds. Then, at some point, the accumulated momentum begins to work in your favor and a breakthrough occurs. The disk gains speed to the point where you no longer have to push as hard. All that is required now to keep the wheel spinning are a few ongoing pushes.

Collins offers a great question: "What was the one big push that caused this thing to go so fast?" There was no one push. It was the collective effort of several pushes, each representing a small fraction of the overall momentum.[3]

Outsiders looking in will never quite understand the hard work required to get the flywheel moving. Insiders will never forget the unified effort of push after push. When the flywheel effect was researched in churches, it was found that struggling churches can experience a breakthrough and ongoing momentum only if they first do the work of a unified effort of buildup.[4]

When the flywheel is at rest, nothing will slow down the church. You're at a standstill! There is little to lose. But the unified effort required to get the flywheel spinning means you have everything to gain. Each push is another paragraph in the comeback story. Each rotation is a chapter. The pace of change may feel slow at first, but you're making progress as long as you continue to push.

Over time, the accumulating momentum becomes the story. Everybody likes a comeback story. People love to cheer for the underdog. As momentum builds, more people will jump in to help push the flywheel. At some point, the momentum will lead to a breakout for the church.

Picking Up the Pace without Knocking the Wind Out of Your Church

Established churches are notorious for hanging on rather than forging ahead. If the church reflects the population age demographics and avoids a mass exodus or a split, the replacement rate of the population will keep the church afloat for years, if not decades.

Let me explain.

According to the CDC, the average annual death rate in the United States is about 0.87 percent, slightly less than nine deaths per thousand people.[5] Thus, a church of 115 people will lose, on average, one person per year to death. If the families in the church average one birth per year, the replacement rate is 1:1 and overall attendance numbers will remain static. But that church is simply treading water. Even if the church loses two people per year, who stop attending for whatever reason, it would take about twenty-nine years for the church to decline by half—the type of generation-long fade that eventually causes people to wonder, *What happened?*

The pandemic of 2020 caused a seismic shift for a lot of congregations, and many that had been treading water suddenly realized it was now *change or die*.[6] As a sense of urgency settles onto your congregation, you can pick up the pace without knocking the wind out of your church.

Here's how.

First, make prayer the top priority. Change requires wisdom. Ask for wisdom, as God instructs in James 1:5. Discernment is required for leading a church through change. The value of all the leadership books in the world pales in comparison to the power of prayer. You must depend on God as you lead your church through urgent change. If prayer moves mountains, it can also soften the hearts of resistant church members.

Second, lead by example with evangelism. Evangelism apathy is one of the top reasons for a prolonged church decline. When the outward focus wanes, the church inevitably looks inward and becomes gradually more selfish. Pastors must feel a sense of urgency about their own personal evangelism before their church will sense an urgency about turning outward.

Third, show love when tested. One of the hardest parts of leading a church is responding in love. You build credibility with grace, not defensiveness. I've never had a church member commend me for how I picked apart someone's argument. But I've heard many church members commend their pastors for how they responded to criticism with grace.

Fourth, be prophetic without blaming others. Dying churches need a wake-up call. They don't need finger-pointing. Frankly, it doesn't matter how the church got into a death spiral. Soldiers in the heat of battle don't sit around discussing geopolitics. They unite and fight. Your church does not need an exhumation of the past to determine who is to blame. Your church needs a fiery coach to unite the people around a common cause.

One of the best ways to pick up the pace without losing your people is to pitch change with a trial period. Ask your church to allow the change for one year. Change-resistant members can be comforted knowing the intrusion into their comfort zones may not be permanent. At the end of the trial period, one of three decisions can be made: (1) extend the trial period to allow for further evaluation; (2) reverse the change; or (3) make the change permanent. If you end up choosing the last option, it's typically because the benefits of the change have become obvious to most people. Honestly, after a year, most people will not even remember the change effort. Ask them and they will say, "This is the way it's always been."

Keep your focus. Your church can make a comeback. Perspective is important. And it's the subject of the next chapter.

5

Perspective

Managing Expectations

IN THE INTRODUCTION, I explained how optimism always bends toward hope. Sometimes it's difficult to maintain this posture when you're in a storm facing critics and crises. But Jesus not only offers hope *in* the storm, sometimes hope rides in *on* the storm.

In John 6, Jesus is at the height of his ministry. After two years of teaching and performing miracles, his popularity is soaring. A massive crowd witnesses him feeding more than five thousand people from just five loaves and two fish.

Imagine their reaction. *He can make food!* The people could literally taste his miracles.

Jesus is so popular at this point that the people are ready

to take him by force and make him king. But what does Jesus do? He goes down to the shoreline and tells the disciples to get in a boat and go to the other side of the Sea of Galilee. Then Jesus dismisses the crowd and goes up into the hills alone to pray.

Imagine the disciples' disillusionment. Two years of building popularity. Everyone wants Jesus to be king. They would be his first-tier leaders in a new kingdom. The problem was that everyone wanted Jesus for what he could *do* for them rather than wanting Jesus himself.

As the disciples get in the boat and head across the lake, a storm builds—a common occurrence on the Sea of Galilee. The geography of the region—with the lake almost seven hundred feet below sea level, surrounded by hills rising close to two thousand feet—creates a meteorological effect. Cool air pushing down from the hills collides with warm air over the water and churns the sea.

Around three o'clock in the morning, Jesus finishes praying and takes a stroll out onto the lake to meet his disciples on the other side. The boat at this point is still far from shore, battered by the waves, and the men are bone tired. When they see Jesus walking on the water toward them, they freak out. They think he is a ghost.[1]

Why would Jesus do this? He is teaching them a critical lesson about hope. Faith does not grow when life is easy. Faith grows when we experience trials, when we are tested, when a storm hits. Trials may be the way God accomplishes his purposes in our lives. To know the strength of something, we must test it. To know the strength of our faith, it must be tested.

Was Peter impetuous when he got out of the boat and started walking on the water toward Jesus? Was he nuts? No. Jesus invited him out. Jesus never invites us to do anything sinful or wrong. What drove Peter was simple: He loved Jesus and wanted to be with him. Peter trusted Jesus. Peter had been *in* a boat in a storm many times. This was his first time *out* of the boat in a storm. You don't build character by repeating the same test over and over again. You build character by stretching people to do things they've never done before. The test was harder than Peter anticipated. He started sinking in fear, but Jesus was right there.

Jesus sent the disciples to a place where they would feel apart from him. Jesus did not minimize the storm; he maximized himself and his presence. Jesus sends us into storms so we will understand the weight of God's glory and the urgency of his mission. There is hope amid the storm. But hope also rides in on the storm.

As you begin to revitalize your church, you and your congregation will be battered by waves. As a leader, you will reach the point of exhaustion. But perhaps God is preparing you to do something you've never done before.

The third part of the revitalization checklist includes managing expectations. *Are your expectations properly aligned?* In most cases, a church's desires are far removed from what is most beneficial. Additionally, congregational expectations rarely align with leadership expectations.

Warfare against Discouragement

Discouragement is inevitable, but it does not have to be debilitating. Be realistic. Take a moment and pray. How discouraged are you? Pastors can bury their discouragement like garbage in a landfill. It remains unseen until eventually the mound rises to a point where people start asking, "What is that?" Use this five-point scale to rate the intensity of your current level of discouragement.

1. I enjoy pastoring my church and can't imagine being anywhere else.
2. At times I have doubts, but I feel supported by my church.
3. If another opportunity came my way, I would consider it.
4. I'm weary and want to start putting out my résumé.
5. I can't take it anymore. I'm about to quit.

Use the scale below to rate how often you feel discouraged.

1. I never feel discouraged.
2. I rarely feel discouraged.
3. I sometimes feel discouraged.
4. I often feel discouraged.
5. I always feel discouraged.

Multiply your two scores. For example, if you marked a 2 on the first scale and a 3 on the second scale, your final score is 6. If your final score is 9 or higher, you are likely in an unhealthy place of ongoing stress. The higher your score, the unhealthier your stress level.

All church revitalization work will become discouraging at some point. These churches need help for a reason. The people are cranky. The facility is falling apart. The financial outlook is bleak. The church's reputation is sour. The programs are dated. The disunity is ongoing. In a way, you should expect discouragement. But you must also battle against it.

Andrew Davis describes this warfare in his book on church revitalization:

> The tension was so thick I could barely catch my breath or walk steadily to preach. The text was not a particularly difficult passage, but I was preaching to so many hate-filled faces that I found myself clutching the sides of the pulpit just to keep upright. After barely making it through that sermon, I went home to recuperate for the evening service. I lay down in a hammock out in the backyard and prayed . . . and cried.[2]

You don't need to know the context to believe what he wrote because you likely have felt the same way. Andrew walked into the church conference the following Wednesday with a renewed perspective:

In common language, we would lose the battle at our church conference but win the war for church revitalization. I went to work as usual on Monday morning, but the staff all saw a noticeable change in my demeanor. I was happy, confident, and excited about what was going to happen long term."[3]

The church vote didn't go the way he wanted, but God gave him a fresh vision for the future.

Nothing to Lose: Using Low Expectations to Your Advantage

Low expectations are often a silent killer in the church. In low-expectation churches, the back door is often as large, if not larger, than the front door. One of the keys to assimilating people into your church for the long haul is raising expectations.[4] When you emphasize a commitment to groups, serving, giving, and faithful attendance, you tend to attract people who desire a high-expectation culture and train others to rise to the level of a high-expectation culture.

The problem is that struggling churches tend to *lower* the bar of expectations, thinking it will stem the tide of losses. But low expectations only make things worse, creating a vicious cycle in which the struggling church no longer attracts or keeps people. Only the most faithful loyalists remain. Often they can't even articulate *why* the church exists.

When you inherit a church in a state of fragile resiliency, the low-expectation culture is often expressed as exhaustion, bitterness, or both. Some in the church will exhibit a self-righteous exhaustion, claiming they are the only ones working in the church (while at the same time not allowing others to help). Others in a struggling low-expectation church will display a self-induced bitterness, choosing to see the worst in the people who left and the worst in the surrounding community.

"They left, so I don't like them."

"They won't visit our church, so I don't like them."

What I'm describing may seem extreme, but many struggling churches are characterized by exhaustion and bitterness to some degree.

Historically, "death trap churches" only attracted pastors who were desperate, ignorant, or way ahead of their time in the field of church revitalization. Today more pastors and church leaders are willing to try to turn these struggling churches around. Why? If God can save any person, he can save any church. Even so-called death traps are worth the effort because they are part of the Kingdom of God. They are worth the effort because the communities where they are located deserve a strong gospel presence.

Though in many cases the prospects in these churches are dire, they are not hopeless. Outsiders aren't expecting much, so any forward progress is amplified. Insiders have not experienced success in years, so any movement has a greater impact on them.

I once consulted with a church whose drug-addicted pastor preached the same sermon every week for two years. That is not an exaggeration. The congregation didn't know what to do, so they simply tolerated the incompetence. Finally, the pastor stopped showing up to preach, and the church woke up from two years of doing nothing.

Their next step changed everything. The church rallied twenty people and served the community through Vacation Bible School. It wasn't the program that saved the church. It was focusing on and doing one thing.

The key to snapping out of a low-expectation environment is to focus the church on *one* effort. One unified effort can start to move the flywheel and create momentum. When we went door-to-door at my first church, it was the first outreach into the community in years. Even so, we did it so poorly that we know God alone brought us success.

Many churches are busy, complex, and moving in too many different directions. The benefit of having nothing to lose is that *one effort* can change the direction of the church. As a leader in a low-expectation environment, you also have the opportunity to *focus* in a way that larger, busier churches cannot. The simplicity of focus does not mean it's easy, but in a struggling church, the rewards of one effort are magnified.

Three Bad Dreams and the Killer Known as Pessimism

During a low moment at a previous church, I put together a spreadsheet of all the places I thought I could live. I weighed the pros and cons and sought God in prayer about each location. I dreamed about someplace new. I dreamed about a new congregation. I dreamed about a fresh start. One place rose to the top. When I shared the epiphany with my wife, she took one look at the location and said, "We're not called there."[5] A strong dose of reality helped assign my heart to the proper place. My dreams were misguided. Had I followed my dream, my life would have become a nightmare.

There is no better place than where you are right now. Maybe you're like me: constantly restless. In my mind, there is always a better place, and it's not always related to geography. Optimists are often haunted by questions of better. *How can I do better? What can I do better? Why don't others want something better?* These questions are not bad ones to ask, unless they move you away from the mission of your present place. Don't confuse perfectionism with optimism. Perfectionism is a killer of optimism. Perfectionism sets the bar so high that any achievement is a disappointment.

Bad Dream #1: Another Location

Stop dreaming about a better location! God has your church right where he wants you. God sovereignly ordained your address. Cherish it. Own it. Believe in and commit yourself to the mission at your location.

Several years ago, I did a research project on large legacy churches.[6] Their facilities are some of the most impressive in the nation. Their locations are the envy of other churches—hundreds of acres of prime real estate in large metropolitan areas.

In one interview I asked a key leader, "What's next? You have accomplished so much. Where is God leading you now?"

I will never forget his answer: "We need to replace the carpet in the hallways. It will cost more than a million dollars."

Bemoaning the funds required to support the massive facility, he said the resource dump back into the location was beginning to wear on the people faster than the people wore out the carpet.

"If we built today, we would not build the size and magnitude of what we have built and have to maintain. We have 750,000 square feet of property, sixteen acres of carpet that not only has to be vacuumed every week but also must be maintained."

Many pastors view this church's campus and location as a dream spot. But it has become a nightmare for those trying to maintain it. Do not get swept into location envy. You have your perfect spot. Dreaming about someone else's location will only create pessimistic nightmares for you.

Bad Dream #2: Another Community

Stop dreaming about a different community! It's only a distraction from the ministry at hand. Whereas Bad Dream #1 focuses on the physical features of your church's campus, *community* refers to the people. Dreaming about a different community—that is, a different group of people to serve—is simply disobedience to your calling. Take this dream too far and you may end up in Tarshish.

Jonah was a successful prophet serving a successful king. Through God's guidance, Jonah prophesied that King

Jeroboam II would restore Israel's northern border.[7] But Jonah got another prophetic mission terribly wrong. In the book that bears his name, he becomes the villain, the anti-missionary.

When God clearly tells Jonah, "Get up and go to the great city of Nineveh," the prophet replies, "Yeah, no," and gets on a boat going the opposite direction.[8]

What was the great city of Nineveh like? The people were depraved and thoroughly wicked. Their warriors were known to rip the lips off the faces of their enemies. They severed hands from arms. They made great piles of skulls as trophies. Jonah not only feared for his life, he also believed the people of Nineveh were not worthy of redemption.

Dreaming of another community will become a self-induced nightmare. You are called to reach the people around you. You're lying to yourself if you think, *I can't reach these people*. It's also a lie to think, *I could reach other people better*. You are called by *God* to reach the people around you.

I doubt you are as disobedient as Jonah or your community is as wicked as Nineveh. The story of Jonah is an extreme case; but it's also a cautionary tale. The fish spit up Jonah after God put him in a three-day time-out. It's hard to connect to your community when you're covered in vomit. Jonah was pessimistic about the Ninevites. Pessimism is vomit on God's mission. Avoid the journey to the bottom of the sea and start dreaming about ways to reach your neighborhood.

Bad Dream #3: Another Time
Stop dreaming about a past era! Longing for a different time is the most wasteful dream of all. God hasn't called you to the past. He never does. Dreaming of the past is about as satisfying as eating a week-old donut. It may look enticing for a moment, but the moment you take a bite you realize you have made a grave mistake. Dreaming of a past era is nothing more than selfish revisionist history. Any glowing memories you have of a past era are inherently biased. Nothing will make you more pessimistic about the present than an idealized dream of the past.

Pessimism is a killer for any church or ministry. Sometimes it comes in the form of dreams. We like to dream as an escape, but too often the escape becomes a trap of pessimism. There are better dreams. Dreams that will pull you toward optimism.

Three Good Dreams and the Optimism of Where You Are Now

You are in the right place at the right time with the right people. Having the right perspective means realizing that, until he moves you, God has you right where he wants you. It's easy to lose this sense of rootedness amid the fog of ministry. Dream about what God can do with you and the people of your church, right here and right now.

Good Dream #1: Right Here
Optimistic pastors dream about what God can do in their location. Church leaders should love their community as

much as they love their church. Granted, some churches are easier to love than others, and some communities are easier to love than others. A calling to a place, however, requires a love for that place. Love for a congregation mismatched with disdain for a community will cause you to retreat into an unhealthy church bubble. Either you will lead your congregation inward, or they will (rightly) question your bitterness and lack of outward focus.

A good dream *always* becomes a reality. A good dream is a God-given dream—one rooted in who he is. Psalm 37:4 conveys an important truth: God will give you the desires of your heart. Context is key here. God doesn't promise to grant whatever comes to your mind. He only grants desires that grow out of our delight in him—desires in which he is the object. If you desire what God desires, any dream you have will become a reality.

Far too often, we rely on feelings to guide our dreams. Feelings fail us because our hearts deceive us. Jeremiah 17:9 leaves a lingering question: Who really knows how bad the human heart is? Frankly, I don't want to find out, and I would encourage you not to test the depravity of your own heart.

Start pursuing God's mission—*doing* the actions of love—and he will give you the desires of your heart. And the feelings will follow.

If your current location is away from home, don't jump at every opportunity, or fabricate lame excuses, to get back home. Devote your heart to the place where God has called you. God calls church leaders to minister in a place. If you're looking for any and every chance to leave that place, you're likely not being a good gospel ambassador in your current posting.

Every community has unique ways (or occasions) it celebrates. Jump in and contribute to the celebration. Only the most hardened curmudgeon can hang on to bitterness when everyone else is having fun.

Live with the people. Don't move to the outskirts; live in the heart of your community. Your home is not a retreat from ministry; it is a crucial asset in ministry. Stop complaining. It's difficult to grow a church when you're known as the town killjoy. Stay active. Be on the go in your community. Sluggishness exacerbates loneliness, frustration, displeasure. Join a civic organization. Be a leader beyond your church. When the community at large is looking to you for leadership, you are obligated to create a positive outlook for everyone.

Good Dream #2: Right Now

Optimistic pastors dream about what God can do right now. Great leaders are typically organizers and communicators of vision. They inspire with their plans for the future. Just as important as a grand vision, however, is a grand appreciation for the moment at hand. Embrace the power of *right now*. The creative fuel of vision can diminish when leaders do not embrace the power of spontaneity. Many of my most creative moments have come by accident when I experienced something unplanned or unexpected.

Without creativity, it is difficult to inspire people with a vision for the future. A sense of levity enhances leadership. Church leaders who learn to laugh and joke spontaneously can be accepted as more genuine, authentic, and enjoyable.

Most importantly, when God's people embrace the power of right now, God can provide incredible opportunities to help connect people to Jesus. As believers, we should pray daily that God will put people in front of us who need to hear the only true message of reconciliation and joy. By embracing the power of right now, you just might see God work in the moment.

Good Dream #3: Right People

Optimistic pastors dream about God using the existing people in the church. Love your church where they are today, not a future, idealized version of your church. Love the congregants you have now, not the ones you wish you had. The decision to love today is more important than the ability to lead in the future.

Pete is a pastor in the North Country of New York State, just south of the Canadian border. He inherited a mess of a church. In one of our coaching calls, I could sense his frustration.

"Am I really doing anything?"

He wasn't blaming his church. He was self-assessing.

I had a hard time responding because there were no easy answers. If his church were a biblical character, it would be Gomer. How many times can you endure a love betrayed?

"You are doing something," I told him. "You're learning to love, and loving people is not inactivity."

When you sit with your spouse and simply enjoy each other, many could look at the scene and claim, "They are doing nothing." But the opposite is true. In that moment, everything is happening. Learning to love is one of the most precious acts pastors can do for their churches. The effort of love can only produce an optimistic mindset. It's impossible to be pessimistic when you are genuinely attempting to love.

Stop asking God, "Where are you?" God is always where he needs to be. In Jeremiah 2:6, Israel is accused of apostasy. God laments a love betrayed. One of his complaints is that Israel stopped asking where he was. "They did not ask, 'Where is the LORD?'"

My own children can become annoying with the constant question, "Where are you, Dad?" If my wife is gone for more than thirty minutes, my youngest daughter will call for her incessantly: "Mom, where are you?"

But what if our children stopped asking? What if they stopped caring about our whereabouts? Their lack of concern would point to a departure of love. It would crush my wife and me. God laments when you stop caring about where he is. God is concerned when you stop asking where he is.

Where is God? He's hanging out at your address.

He's waiting for you to seek him.

6

People

The Church's Capacity to Move Forward

God's blessing is one of the most misunderstood concepts in the Bible. It's also one of the most misapplied ideas in our lives. We assume we know how God wants to bless us. We assume we know what God's blessings look like. We want the blessing on our terms, in our way, and within our sense of proper timing.

The book of Haggai closes with God promising to bless the people: "From this day onward I will bless you."[1] What an ending to the story! But the journey to this point was not the easiest path. God's blessings are ultimately not about the good life, a vibrant ministry, successful children, or a pay raise. God's blessings can also come in the form of hard nights, tears, and funerals. Pain and loss can unravel us, but pain and loss can also transform us. James writes, "God blesses those who patiently endure testing."² As your church begins to move forward, not everything will feel like a blessing. In fact, the blessings may feel more like testing.

The fifth century BC was a dreary period in Israel's history. The empire of David and Solomon had crumbled. The Assyrians had destroyed the northern kingdom. Nebuchadnezzar and the Babylonians had ransacked the southern kingdom, including Jerusalem. Haggai and his people had been carted hundreds of miles away from their homeland. Later, when the Persians rose to power, King Cyrus allowed the people of Israel to return to their homes. Haggai went back with Zerubbabel, the governor, and Joshua, the high priest. What they found in Jerusalem was shocking. The city had been plundered. The Temple was a pile of stones. Undeterred, they started rebuilding, only to be discouraged by the enormity of the task.

A quasi-slogan emerged among the people: "The time has not yet come to rebuild the house of the LORD."³ In other words, *just do it* became *just wait*.

God was unimpressed with their spiritual procrastination. They were taking his name in vain to justify their selfishness. But don't we do the same thing? We tell God, "You can work in my life when I'm ready." God does not bless us when we invoke his name as justification for our laziness.

After a series of wake-up calls from God, the people stopped working on their own homes and started working on rebuilding God's house.⁴

Still, they had to fight through discouragement. The previous Temple had been far superior. King Solomon had utilized 200,000 people over seven years to construct a true wonder of the world, filled with gold, silver, and fine stone. Now it was rubble, and the new Temple would never match the grandeur of the old one. Haggai and Zerubbabel had only 50,000 people and few of the resources used in building the previous Temple. Their capacity to build was limited, but God had bigger plans.

You may feel the same about your church. Maybe there was a golden era in the past when hundreds more attended and nice buildings were constructed through a series of successful capital campaigns. Now the church is in disrepair. The few people remaining are tired, if not selfishly focused on their own agendas.

Now you have a taste of how Haggai felt.

The fourth part of the checklist includes understanding your church's capacity for change and helping them move forward.

What is their true capacity to move forward?

It's a key question, but there's another one you must answer first: Are you willing to love your people where they are now?

Loving Your Church Right Now

Optimistic leaders will love their church right where it is now, not some future version of the church. There is no upside if you despise the church when she is down. You must love people where they are to help guide them where they need to be. If you don't love your church where they are today, you'll never muster the faith and love it will take to lead them to the other side of tomorrow. You have the exact people and resources you need right now to begin accomplishing God's goal for your church. You might have to get creative if you are limited in numbers and finances, but you have access to all the creative energy you need in God himself.

Few churches are truly healthy. Most congregations need work in at least one area, if not several. Part of loving your church right now is accurately assessing the current state of the congregation. Several metrics point to declining or improving church health. Worship attendance, giving, conversions, and Bible study involvement are all common ways to gauge the health of a congregation. But what these metrics can miss is the overall health of the culture. Here are four questions that can help you begin to peel back the layers of your church's culture.

1. *Is your church engaged or unengaged with the community?* This answer is relatively easy to find. Take an afternoon and go to local businesses, make a purchase, and then ask the cashier about your church. The question can be as simple as "What do you know about First Community Church?" The answers will be telling.

   I recently consulted with a large church in the mid-South. Almost none of the parishioners lived in the community. The church has a large campus that sits high on a hill. The steeple is the tallest visible structure in the community. I walked across the street to a gas station and asked the cashier about the church. He had no clue and said he had never heard of it. I pointed out the window at the massive campus and mentioned to him about the church. He shrugged his shoulders and said, "I don't think I've ever paid much attention to it."

2. *Is your church willing to change, or are people entrenched in how things have always been?* Resistance to change is one of the largest hurdles in leadership. A key to understanding this resistance is recognizing the type of change you are recommending. Most people want pastors to work on technical changes: getting better curriculum, fixing the air conditioning, improving the campus, preaching sermons with better illustrations. Few people desire cultural changes that will challenge the status quo. There is a reason why some things get embedded in the culture of a church. Most people find them acceptable. Many churches do not believe cultural change is necessary. Many churches resist change because they do not believe it is feasible. Many churches resist change because it reshuffles the power alignment. You must love your church right now to have any chance of leading the people through change.

3. *Is your church hungry or desperate for a solution?* Hunger implies a healthy appetite. Desperation can lead to rash decisions. A hungry church may not know what is healthy, but at least the people are demonstrating a desire to be fed. Desperation leads to poor decisions about hiring a pastor, selling the campus, or merging with another church. Even desperate churches deserve to have a loving pastor. But showing love to desperate people requires a firmness about the right direction for the church. A hungry church can take small bites. A desperate church needs explicit instructions.

4. *Is your church stable or on life support?* Not every situation is a crisis. I remember talking to a young pastor who thought his church would collapse unless they agreed to a slate of immediate changes. When I looked at the giving and attendance trends, I pointed out that his church had not changed in thirty years. That's not good, but it's also not a crisis. Stability can become entrenchment. Plenty of churches are stuck. But they don't need crisis management; they need a slow winch out of the mud. Loving your church right now means not overreacting as a leader.

How can you determine the capacity of your church to move forward? The following diagnostic tool is a good place to start.

The Capacity Formula

Chapter 4 covered the pace of change, which involves speed. How fast can the church adapt and change? This next part of the revitalization checklist is about capacity. Capacity involves ability. How capable is the church of moving forward? The capacity filter is a simple way to gain a general understanding of your church's ability to handle change. As you answer the three questions below, be as accurate in your numbers as possible. If your church is smaller, work with the names of the people in each category. If your church is larger, do your best to make accurate estimates.

Answer the questions with numbers, not percentages.

1. How many people are active in your church?

2. How many supportive leaders are in your church?

3. How many malcontents are in your church?

Active people are ones who attend your church at least twice a month. Supporters are those who are not only active but also willing to champion your vision for the church. Malcontents are those who are openly opposed to change or those who will complain behind the scenes to derail your vision for the church. Many people in your church, if not the majority, will be neither supporters nor malcontents. In most churches, most people go with the flow. Once you have figures for each of these three groups, plug them into the formula below and solve for X, which will give you a percentage.

(Supporters minus Malcontents) ÷ Active People = X

With this percentage, you can understand where your church stands in terms of capacity. Few churches have a percentage of active supporters greater than thirty-one percent, mainly because most people in the church are not active supporters or active detractors. This dynamic will be covered more in the next section. For now, use the following categories to assess your church.

- Low capacity: 10 percent or less
- Average capacity: 11–20 percent
- High capacity: 21–30 percent
- Unusual capacity: 31 percent or greater

Low-capacity churches typically have short-tenured pastors and a history of conflict. There may have been a split in the recent past. Often these churches have an older congregation with members whose default posture is cynicism. They are not hopeless or beyond repair, but leading them will take endurance and a willingness to face some heat. If the malcontents outnumber the supporters, the percentage will be negative. Unfortunately, most churches with a negative percentage will not survive, as there are not enough supporters to gain momentum over the malcontents. Low-capacity churches rarely grow.

Average-capacity churches are not without conflict, but enough supporters exist to gain traction. At least one ministry in these churches is likely to be thriving. Many times, it is the children's ministry or student ministry, which can be insulated from other problem areas in the church. Average capacity churches have a typical rate of pastoral turnover, rotating through pastors every five years or so. In many cases, a few families make up the core of the church supporters and act as a buffer, preventing major conflict. An average capacity church may be in decline or experiencing replacement growth, where enough new people come in to replace those who leave.

High-capacity churches will have multiple successful ministries. The pastor is typically beyond the often turbulent third or fourth year of tenure. These churches will have a unified staff. Unless there is a demographic barrier, these churches are growing steadily and assimilating new people. A spirit of unity defines these congregations. Though conflict can occur, it is quickly extinguished before a fire can begin to rage.

Churches with unusual capacity typically have a long-term pastor with a string of successful initiatives over several years. Most churches will never reach this level of capacity, much less maintain it over time. If your church fits this category, you can take some calculated risks, but be careful not to abuse the high levels of trust. Unusual capacity churches will almost always grow rapidly as the number of supporters in the church far outweigh any malcontents. The people have an expectation of growth. New people join because they want to support the vision and direction of the church. Churches with unusual capacity should be willing to help other churches in the area and share their resources. One way to see your church drop out of this category is to hoard people and resources as other churches in the area decline. God will not honor a church with unusual capacity that does not attempt to multiply, plant, and revitalize.

Four Ways to Prepare for Increased Capacity

Haggai faced a difficult challenge: how to motivate a discouraged people to do a God-sized task for which they had few resources. The stone-by-stone process was slow. One month into the work, the people wanted to stop again. A group of naysayers started murmuring about the glories of the past and how the future was not going to be as good. Even when they had worked on the Temple foundation sixteen years before, this group wept and wailed among those celebrating progress.[5] Haggai heard the same thing you might hear.

"It's not like it used to be."

"We'll never get back to where we were."

"I miss our church from years ago."

Two groups of people worked on the Temple: those who believed the past was more glorious and those who were excited about seeing God work in the present. If you lean toward the camp of the past being better, I urge caution. We cannot love the church of the past more than the church of the future. In fact, I can guarantee you are outside God's will if you love the past more than the future. Two questions will reveal why.

Can anyone be saved in the past? No.

Will anyone be saved in the future? Yes.

Memories are precious. Nostalgia is good, to a point. But worshiping the past is idolatry. God reminds the people around Haggai that he will shake the nations, that the treasures of the world belong to him. The people didn't have the resources. God did. When God builds his church, he will provide.

God increased their capacity to build the Temple. He can increase your church's capacity as well. How can you prepare your soul for this increased capacity? Leaders can start the process of increased capacity with four biblical postures: *humility*, *humor*, *history*, *courage*. Get ready to see God work.

Humility

When faced with hostility, respond with humility. Keep Ephesians 6:12 close at hand: "We are not fighting against flesh-and-blood enemies, but against evil rulers and authorities of the unseen world, against mighty powers in this dark world, and against evil spirits in the heavenly places."

Unfortunately, Satan plants "double agents" in churches to stir up division.[6] Humility is one way to root them out. Light is a far more powerful force than darkness. We should not fight darkness with other darkness but rather with light. Humility is a force of light.

When you respond without pride and with gentleness, it can prompt others to discern truth. But when you rile up others to join your fight, you can confuse people and cloud their judgment. Obviously, you should not tolerate attacks against doctrine or family. In cases where the nonnegotiables of the faith are compromised, you are justified in an elevated response, though always with grace and humility. The reality is that most fights in the church are about preferences. Do not make yourself a lightning rod over preferences. The personal virtue of humility is a constant battle, but an important one. Humility is a daily decision and a lifetime commitment. God increases capacity through humble leaders and removes capacity with prideful leaders.

Humor

When faced with agitation, respond with humor. Social cohesion is formed through humor, and not enough leaders use humor intentionally. Humor helps people cope with difficult dilemmas and is an immediate and long-term coping mechanism.[7] One of the best forms of humor is self-deprecation, which complements humility. Rather than trying to land an edgy joke, refer to your own shortcomings in a way that disarms people. When people are agitated, you might be the recipient but not the cause of the agitation. Helping people laugh will put them in a better frame of mind and will also make them view you more positively. Humor is a way to build trust without taking risks. It's also a way to be more friendly and approachable as a church leader and pastor. The more your church enjoys your presence, the more people will move into a supportive posture. As support grows for the leaders, so does the capacity of the church.

History

When faced with stubbornness, respond with history. In my late twenties, I pastored a church with a historical marker and a 200-page book dedicated to its history. A key part of loving the congregation was knowing the history. I read the book several times and studied the archives of the church. It was a way to demonstrate love. I made a lot of leadership mistakes there, but at least the church knew I had a genuine love of their past. The only way forward was by knowing the past.

Celebrate the parts of the past that support the future vision. You become what you celebrate, and there are plenty of things to celebrate in the past that will push you into the future. Tell the story of past change efforts with a positive perspective. Denigrating the past will taint the future. Having a negative perspective of past change efforts will not help you craft a vision. Utilize positive past change efforts and tell that story.

Turn the legacy into a guide, not a hurdle. Legacy can either be negative or positive. Not everything in the past is worth celebrating. But even the negative parts of a church's history can become a guide, not a hurdle. You will not know how to take corrective action unless you acknowledge past mistakes. And you can't acknowledge past mistakes unless you know the history of the church. You can honor the past while not losing sight of the future. In fact, the honor you show the past may become the way in which future capacity opens up.

Courage

When faced with uncertainty, respond with courage. Capacity cannot expand without a pastor's courage. The powers of darkness will not cede territory without a fight. You will face uncertainty with job security. You will face uncertainty with church finances. You will face uncertainty because of spiritual warfare. Courage is rooted in the understanding that our reward is great in heaven even if our earthly battles are grueling.

Following a cantankerous meeting of Baptist leaders, the young William Carey formed a mission society. At the inaugural meeting, he preached a sermon and made a bold call: "Expect great things; attempt great things."[8]

Carey went to India in the late 1790s and lost everything, including one of his children. Yet the torturous season was marked by the assurance of God's presence:

"This is indeed the valley of the shadow of death to me. . . . But I rejoice that I am here, notwithstanding; and God is here, who . . . is able to save to the uttermost."[9]

Carey saw the believers of his time as far too at ease with a lost world. His words echo those of Amos 6:1. "What sorrow awaits you who lounge in luxury." Christian leaders often speak out about the negative cultural influences of the entertainment industry and social media, but the dullness of apathy and complacency are the true satanic influences in our society.

Carey considered himself a plodder, who could "persevere in any definite pursuit."[10] Indeed, he plodded for seven years before baptizing his first convert in India. By the time he died, he had spent forty-one years in India without a furlough. He translated the Bible into India's major languages, led major social reforms, helped abolish infanticide and widow burning, and founded a college that also served as a divinity school and still exists today. In many ways, he was a flawed missionary, but what made him stand apart was his courage. God increased the capacity of his work because he pushed forward courageously.

Hope Looks Forward to God's Future

I led my first mission trip as a lead pastor when I was in my midtwenties. As I drove the church bus to our destination, I was filled with grand expectations. Much like the Hebrew people returning to Jerusalem with Haggai, my hopes were high and my spirits were up.

When we arrived in New Orleans, we found that Hurricane Katrina had ravaged the area in ways we did not expect. At the outset of our journey in Indiana, I had been sure our little group was going to make an immediate impact. Instead, our job in the Lower Ninth Ward was to shovel rubble from a pile inside a church to a pile outside the church. I felt small and useless. The discouragement found in the book of Haggai made more sense.

Then a member of the devastated church approached me. She thanked us. She spoke of the future as if we were rebuilding Solomon's Temple. I wanted to ask her if debris had hit her on the head during the storm. I was wrong. God spoke to me through her. It wasn't about rebuilding the church facility but rather a *reminder* of where we ought to place our hope.

In Haggai, God recognized the obvious. The Temple they were building seemed like nothing compared to Solomon's Temple. But then God made a promise: "The future glory of this Temple will be greater than its past glory."[11] God was building something more than the physical structure of the Temple. The greater work would culminate in Jesus. He would physically enter the Temple they were building and become the fulfilment of it. They were not taking downward steps; they were taking steps up!

Maybe the grandeur of your church's past haunts you. Perhaps people remind you of a historical era long gone. Don't get discouraged. God is building your hope. There is a final glory. Jesus will get you to that place.

7

Place

The Issue of Facilities

THE ELEPHANT IN THE ROOM *is* the room. For many mega-churches, the centerpiece attraction has become an albatross. Large churches with megafacilities are finding the space harder and harder to fill.

The first time I walked into the worship space of one of my favorite megachurches, the room took my breath away—three tiers and a seating capacity of five thousand. Their lobby area has the same square footage as the entire campus of my current church. At the time this megachurch campus was built, big was the way to go. Many of these giant campuses—some as large as 500,000 square feet—were built just before the multisite movement picked up steam. The prevailing wisdom at the time was to build large and fill the room. Unfortunately, the strategy has not worked as well as church leaders hoped. Many have discovered that the cost of maintaining their facility is a far greater burden than the original cost of building the campus.

We have learned that unlimited growth is a myth. No church can expand infinitely upward, because God designed the church to multiply outward. These megachurches are reminders that the facility must match the mission. Some churches can grow to five or ten thousand people, and their facilities may match their God-given calling. But not every church will grow that large or that fast. Not every church needs a five-thousand-seat sanctuary.

Maintaining megachurch campuses will become even more of a problem in the future. However, a greater, more expensive problem looms now. The financial liability of all the smaller church campuses in disarray far overshadows the few megachurch campuses that are not being filled. Dying churches are a waste of resources and prime locations. Revitalized churches are efficient uses of Kingdom resources. For the megachurch, the elephant in the room *is* the room. For the tens of thousands of dying churches, the elephant in the room is all the empty rooms combined. *Is your church facility ready for revitalization?* From a financial perspective, this part of the checklist is paramount.

The Most Prominent Discipleship Tool

The church campus is not the most important discipleship tool, but it is often the most prominent. The building is not the church, but it is hard to be the church without a building. Whether you have a permanent location or not, whether you own or lease space, whether the campus is too big or too small, think of your facility's footprint as a discipleship tool. Without the building, fewer people would attend worship gatherings. Without the building, fewer people would go to small group studies. Without the building, my church's partnership with a local day school could not happen.

During the COVID-19 pandemic, many churches realized the power of a digital presence. Pastors scrambled to go online. Viewership spiked, then crashed. A digital footprint is necessary to operate as a church today, but a digital-first strategy will create only consumers of content, not disciples.

Is a church building *necessary* for discipleship? Absolutely not. But the gathering of the saints is essential. This gathering is designed by God to be in person. A church that does not gather—in person—does not exist. The church building is the top facilitator for allowing this gathering to happen.

There is a correlation between a healthy church and adequate facilities. Healthy churches take care of their facilities. Unhealthy churches tend to let their facilities decline.[1] A church's campus tells a story that people *feel*. The appearance of the campus is interwoven with the story of the people who gather onsite.[2] Almost everyone has a connection to a place or a building or a classroom where something special happened. It's why people feel nostalgic about the chapel where they were married or the summer camp cafeteria where they made a commitment to Christ.

From a symbolic perspective, organizations can be assessed as much by appearance as by outcomes. Leaders can create symbols to anchor hope and faith, and leaders who use symbols well can reinforce and shape the culture of their organization.[3] One example of a symbol in an established church is the building itself. The emotional ties to the physical building in these churches are as strong as the relational connection among the congregation. When pastor Adrian Rogers led the relocation of Bellevue Baptist Church in the 1980s, he emphasized from the pulpit the importance of symbolism. "We're taking our memories with us," he said, "and we're taking our chandelier with us, too."[4] His comments were met with a burst of applause.

Longtime church members often identify with the building as much as they do with each other. In this way, church buildings become part of the discipleship process as people connect their spiritual growth to a certain space. Markers in a person's spiritual development may connect with certain parts of buildings and specific classrooms.[5]

The Church Facility Assessment

An easy and practical way to evaluate the health of your church facility is to conduct a simple audit. Ask five longtime church members and five new people to rate ten aspects of your facility on a scale from 1 to 10, where 1 means "totally inadequate" and 10 means "nearly perfect." Have them complete the survey during the week, when they're not in the building, not on a Sunday morning. Tally the scores and compare the answers from the new people to those from the longtime members.

Exterior signage: Is it visible and clearly marked?

1   2   3   4   5   6   7   8   9   10

Parking lot: Is guest and handicap parking evident? Can I navigate the lot easily?

1   2   3   4   5   6   7   8   9   10

Exterior appearance: Does the building look pleasing? Is the landscaping nice?

1   2   3   4   5   6   7   8   9   10

Interior signage: Are there clear directions to each area of the church?

1   2   3   4   5   6   7   8   9   10

General interior appearance: Is the space up to date? Cluttered? Clean? Neat?

1   2   3   4   5   6   7   8   9   10

Worship area/sanctuary: Is it well cared for? Is the setting conducive to worship?

1   2   3   4   5   6   7   8   9   10

Restrooms: Are they in good locations? Clean? Well-supplied? How do they look?

1   2   3   4   5   6   7   8   9   10

Children's area and nursery: Are the toys clean and newer? Would you leave a child here?

1   2   3   4   5   6   7   8   9   10

Student space: Is it age appropriate and clean? How does it look?

1   2   3   4   5   6   7   8   9   10

Hallways and foyer area: Can people gather here? Is it well lighted and inviting?

1   2   3   4   5   6   7   8   9   10

Average the scores for each question and compile into three groups: new people, longtime members, and combined. Compare each total to the following ranges:

10–39: *Bad.* The church facility needs immediate attention and is causing you to lose guests and members.

40–69: *Average.* The church facility is not helping you bring in new people. Start working on the problem areas as soon as you can.

70–89: *Above average.* The church facility has features that are attractive to guests. Work on any problem areas to make your church stand out even more.

90–100: *Exceptional.* Few churches score this high. Your church facility is a major asset to the community and the congregation. Build deferred maintenance items into your budget and maintain your facility so the building does not begin to deteriorate.

If possible, sit down with the respondents one-on-one and ask them to explain their scores in greater depth. The perspective of each group is important, and together they will highlight different aspects of your campus. They will also have different feelings about the church's facilities. These feelings and perceptions are just as important as the facts. Take note of common problem areas and create a priority list to remedy them.

Your Church Address Is Not an Accident

The people in your congregation are not there by accident. Your church's history did not unfold by accident. Maybe you wish you could change all three—new location, new people, and new history. Don't. God has sovereignly placed you where you are. You are leading a particular people with a particular history in a particular location for a reason.

Maybe things need to change in your church. Perhaps a lot needs to change. For most churches, the answer is not a relocation of the campus or trying to squeeze out certain people to make way for a new crowd. And there's nothing you can do to change the history of the church. Church revitalization begins with where you are, the people you have, and the history that brought you there. If God can revitalize any *person*, he can revitalize any *church*. Start with what you have.

Too often, church leadership advice involves new locations, new people, and new stories. What if every church decided to change these three things? The result would be a hopscotch of congregational confusion. *Hey, we're over here now, with new people and a brand-new name on the sign!*

I believe *most* church relocations are unnecessary—and I think they really hurt the Kingdom. The vast majority of churches do not need to change locations, purge existing members, or disregard their history. But for revitalization to happen, something does need to change. Every church is designed to thrive through the power of the Holy Spirit.

My church was founded in 1954. What God began in 1954 is not supposed to stop until Christ returns. The same is true of your church. God has given every church the ability to accomplish his mission at his chosen locations.

The purpose of leadership is to guide people to a better place spiritually. There is no better location to make this happen than right where you are. Your church is where it is because God determined it. Whether your town has a church on every corner or you're in a spiritual wasteland, the sovereignty of God is in your location. Wherever you are. Whatever location you have. Whatever you are experiencing right now. Your church address is not an accident. Start right where you are.

The Church Is a Vehicle, Not a Destination Point

My favorite amusement in Florida is not Disney World. It's the Kennedy Space Center, Florida's gateway to outer space. The historical displays of engineering are impressive—things my mind cannot even grasp—but what I love most about the space center is the story of how the rockets and shuttles that have been launched from the massive complex on Merritt Island fueled the competition (and later, cooperation) between two world powers, the United States and Russia.

Starting around 1955, the space race erupted between the US and the USSR, as both nations announced their intentions to launch satellites into space. Who would get there first? Two years later, America was caught off guard when the Soviets launched Sputnik 1, a beach ball–size satellite, ushering in a new era of political suspicion, military expansion, and scientific achievement.[6] The space age had begun. The backdrop of the Cold War turned this mad dash for technological advancement into a fascinating narrative that captured the imagination of millions for at least the next twenty years.

In 1961, President Kennedy gave a message to a special joint session of Congress. The goal was simple but ambitious: send an American safely to the moon and back before the close of the decade. The scope of the project was enormous. The costs and resources required were comparable to the building of the Panama Canal. But despite some early victories by the Soviets, including the first animal and first human to orbit the earth, the US would not let them win.

Within a few years, American ingenuity had made remarkable advances, and in 1969 Neil Armstrong took one small step for a man and one giant leap for mankind, leaving a footprint of victory on the moon.

I live on the opposite coast of Florida from Cape Canaveral, 135 miles away, but from my yard I can still see rockets launched from the Kennedy Space Center. The night launches are especially noteworthy, as a brilliant trail of fire lights the dark sky.

I've never been in the control room, but I've always imagined they have a giant red button there. So much engineering and planning goes into every launch. Hundreds of people pour weeks and months—if not years—of their lives into a launch moment, and then someone gets to hit that big red button to send the rocket into space.

The ascension of Jesus is the church's giant red button, completing his earthly ministry and launching our mission to continue reaching the world for Christ. During the space race, the mission was clear. It unified everyone. There was a common goal. The church's mission is also clear. There is a common goal. There is a common enemy. Jesus' birth, death, and resurrection get a lot of well-deserved attention. But his ascension is not celebrated nearly as much.

Acts 1:1-11 records a few details of the ascension. The disciples are left gazing up into the sky, until two angels address them and say, "Why are you standing here staring into heaven?"

This moment teaches us something important: Standing

around and gawking is an inappropriate response to the mandate Jesus has given us. Inactive Christians do not grasp the significance of the ascension.

The church is not a destination point for crowds. The church is a vehicle designed by God to take the Good News of Jesus into our neighborhoods, our communities, and ultimately to the nations. You should view your church address as a launchpad. Accomplishing our mission is less about filling the building and more about sending brave saints into the world.

One of my earliest memories involves the *Challenger* explosion. I was in first grade and I remember the excitement surrounding Christa McAuliffe's participation on the mission as the first teacher (and civilian) in space. I remember watching on TV as the Challenger broke apart a mere seventy-three seconds into the launch. I can still see in my mind's eye the grainy images of twisted smoke on the screen and my teacher weeping as she rolled the television out of the classroom.

I've been fascinated with the space shuttle program ever since. Many remember the tragedy of the *Challenger* mission, but what is often overlooked is the incredible success of the space shuttle program in general. The engineering genius behind space shuttles was that they could be reused, returning to earth and landing safely after each mission. The program ultimately included 133 successful missions with five orbiters.[7]

God engineered the local church to send generation after generation on mission. The church is like the space shuttle, the means by which people are sent out repeatedly. Your building, your programs, your polity, and your activities are intended to create an ongoing outward movement that doesn't stop until Christ returns.

Your church is not a destination point for crowds. Your church is a vehicle designed by God with the specific purpose of carrying good news to the nations.

Something New in Someplace Old

The call to shepherd a church is the call to shepherd a community. The mission of the church is the neighborhood. Churches should be planted with the expressed desire of becoming part of the community culture.[8] When a church is planted, one of the key decisions is location, which drives how the church will function and what the church will become. When a church loses its connection to the community, it also loses its reason for being. When pastors stop seeing their role as neighborhood shepherds, it increases the potential that they will begin to see the community as a problem for the church—or worse, an enemy of the church. But in most cases, churches don't become hostile to their community. They simply become indifferent. Satan wins his battles against the church by tempting leaders and congregations with apathy.

Every successful church plant becomes an established congregation. The exciting chaos of newness eventually settles into expected patterns of polity and programs. This settling helps a church maintain its ministry presence. A church *should* settle into a location. Only in rare cases should a church ever leave a location. In a few cases I've seen, an area becomes industrialized and loses its residents. Churches aren't needed where there are no people.

The location of a church is just as important as its doctrine. You can't separate who you are trying to reach (context) from what you believe (doctrine). Abandoning your neighborhood is abandoning your mission. Abandoning your mission is abandoning your theology. Maybe your church is stuck. Maybe you have an older congregation in an older building. But maybe that is less of a disadvantage than you realize. God may be ready to do something new in someplace old.

When a Hurricane Takes It All

One of my favorite churches lost their location in a *force majeure* event.[9] Few experts predicted the ferocity of Hurricane Michael, which slammed into the Florida panhandle in October 2018. Most storms that form in the Caribbean during October end up being weaker systems. Michael turned out to be the fourth-strongest hurricane to hit the United States in recorded history.[10] Mexico Beach, Florida, was wiped off the map. The neighboring town of Port St. Joe sustained massive damage. Hurricane Michael reached Category 5 strength with sustained winds in excess of 160 miles per hour.

For more than twenty years, my family has vacationed in the Port St. Joe area. I went there with my parents when I was younger. Now I make the seven-hour drive from Bradenton with my wife and children. Perhaps you have your own happy place. This one is ours.

Even when I'm on vacation, I still attend church services. I'm not legalistic about it, I simply love the local church—especially established Baptist churches. First Baptist Church Port St. Joe fits the mold. The worship experience there is comfortably nostalgic. The architecture screams mid-century Southern Baptist, and the sanctuary has a familiar smell. It's a time-warp church in a time-warp town. I love every part of this glorious church. The pastor and I are good friends. It's a second church home for me.

Hurricane Michael ripped it all apart. One of the first images I saw after the storm came from the pastor. He texted me a picture of the steeple twisted from its perch and bending toward the ground. Michael treated the church like one of those miniature tchotchkes where the removable roof is a lid. The walls still existed, but the roof was tossed somewhere and forgotten.

Peering inside from above made you question the sovereignty of God. Destruction is a blow like no other. How could a place I love experience such pain? Where was God in the midst of this storm? Frankly, these questions are selfish. But when it affects you directly, that's where your mind goes.

Of course my church in Bradenton helped. Of course we sent people and funds. I am proud of how my primary church home stepped up to help my second church home.

The best in people is sometimes revealed in the most helpless of circumstances.

The First Baptist Port St. Joe's building was ultimately condemned—doomed to demolition. The old familiar place that everyone loved was razed to the foundation. Then the foundation itself was removed—in more ways than one. New building codes meant they could not rebuild on the original site. Now after proclaiming the gospel every Sunday for decades at 102 Third Street, the church had a choice between a funeral or a rebirth. The pastor and people were exhausted, but the labor pains indicated new life that was coming. After one hundred years, the story would continue—not as an additional chapter, but as an entirely new book.

First Baptist Port St. Joe often gives me the honor of preaching when I'm in town. I cherish those moments. One year I stood before them as an evacuee, running from Hurricane Irma as it plowed through my community. The next year, the people of Port St. Joe were the refugees, displaced by Hurricane Michael. The elementary school they now occupied was adequate—in some ways even better. But it wasn't the same. As I prepared to preach that Sunday, God convicted me of selfishness. My feelings came from a place of nostalgia. Did I love *my idea* of their church? Or did I love *God's mission* for their church?

You can't force your way into a future that doesn't exist. You must trust God today with the future he has for you. First Baptist Port St. Joe didn't run. They voted with confidence in the sovereignty of God. In return, he provided something beautiful. New land became available. God gave it to them. Funding came through. God provided the ability to build a new campus.

Every time I drive by the old location, a twinge of nostalgia hits me. All those years at 102 Third Street were not an accident. God wanted decades worth of ministry to happen right there. But neither was Michael an accident. The hurricane became a catalyst for a renewed trust in the sovereignty of God.

Another Great Awakening

Draper and his wife knew God was at work. After several years and two good tenures at churches, something stirred in both of them. But where God called them—one of the oldest Baptist churches in New England—turned out to be uncomfortable.

"But if we are called," Draper said, "we have to let go of our own comfort."

Draper is a native New Englander and the son and grandson of pastors. He's the hardy type of person you'd expect to find in New England. It wasn't the cold winters that made him uncomfortable with his new position. It was a different kind of cold.

When Draper and his wife arrived, the church was not technically closed, but the people had stopped meeting for worship. The previous pastor had experienced some major health issues, and during his illness the church had dwindled to a remnant. Since Draper is bi-vocational, he and his family traveled about a hundred miles three times a week to serve their new church.

Finding a congregation in pain, Draper focused on helping them heal spiritually. They required the Great Physician's touch. Draper shepherded them carefully and lovingly. He soon moved into the parsonage and went all-in. He had a specific goal in mind.

"They needed to fall back in love with Jesus before they could fall in love with reaching the community."

Some members wondered whether the townspeople even liked the church. But the church began to focus and move outward into the community. They started a food pantry. They opened their building to community meetings. They allowed community soccer practices on their field. An outdoors class for kids started on church property.

"The church wondered whether the town liked them," Draper said with a smile. "Well, the town quickly embraced them."

As the church demonstrated Christ's love to their neighbors, God honored their movement outward. The building where the church had not even been gathering was now becoming the hub of the community.

When Draper moved into the parsonage, church attendance actually took a dip—from fifteen people to nine. But after a year of their focusing on evangelism, God began growing the church. Today the church is twenty-five strong and momentum is building. The community is abuzz about what's happening. Men are gathering to pray for the lost.

Women are starting their own prayer meeting. They have begun networking with other church revitalization efforts in the region.

Recently, as the church started renovating the worship space, they encountered some sacred cows. The walls needed paint, but some members were concerned about painting over some familiar features in the sanctuary. Then an old-timer who had helped paint the building many years ago picked up a brush and was the first to start.

"It's not about the building. It's about the people," he said.

With a breath of fresh energy and leadership, what began in the 1730s is not about to stop today. The congregation originally grew out of the events of the Great Awakening. They sponsored George Whitefield when he spoke in the region and shared the gospel across New England. Their first building had been completely burned by the British army during the Revolutionary War.

But they are still there, right where God planted them. God gave them the ability to accomplish his mission at his chosen location. Their address is as important today as it was when they were founded.

"It's something new in someplace old," Draper told me.

The old legacy continues with a new work.

The People and Community

A few years ago, our research team interviewed more than 350 people across the US who were new to church attendance. We asked them about their perceptions of the facilities. Did it affect their decision to attend the church? What they told us was surprising.[11]

The church facility plays an important role in attracting the unchurched. Though some may argue that the church building is of minimal importance, our research came to the opposite conclusion. Different situations call for different types of buildings, styles, venues, and sizes. But the common denominator is this: Excellent church facilities help to attract the unchurched. Church leaders need to take good care of their church facilities in order to maximize their evangelistic efforts.

The church building, however, is not the primary motivating factor for the unchurched. Although the appearance of the building is clearly important in attracting the unchurched, it is not the primary reason these people choose a particular church to attend. More important is the simple fact that someone *invited* them. The main factors in attracting the unchurched are the work of the Holy Spirit in their hearts and the obedience of church members to the Great Commission.

Drive through many towns anywhere in the US and you will find two buildings at the center: the courthouse and a church. Historically, the church has been the central focus of most communities. It was where people congregated to share life's journey.

In many towns and in many ways, the church has lost its place as a community gathering point. Once the center of connection, the church became an ancillary part of the community. The issue of lost fellowship is obviously not a new phenomenon. We notice in the book of Hebrews that some were habitually neglecting the fellowship.[12]

But the subject of community goes much deeper. It is more than just a weekly gathering. It goes beyond the walls of the church. You can't create community by spiritual navel-gazing. Nor does building a gym create community. Even adding a coffee shop won't solve the problem. Churches that become a central focus in their communities have it built into their DNA. It isn't their programs, buildings, or style. Buildings are important, but ultimately it is the *people* of the church who create community.

8

Purpose

Rekindling an Outward Focus

THE CAR SWERVED into the church parking lot. I think it was a mid-80s Ford LTD. The vehicle had seen a lot of wear in its years. The guy who was thrown out of the car looked even worse.

It was late on a Monday evening. I was in a men's small group, and we were the only ones at the church. Our unexpected guest saw the light on and started banging on the floor-to-ceiling glass windows. When we opened the door, the smell told us where he'd spent the last few hours.

Apparently, the Holy Spirit wanted him to come to our group. We served him coffee and asked him to sit with us. Before long, he pointed at me and said, "You must be the preacher. What does the Bible say I should do?"

At the time, I was twenty-two years old, just out of college, and new to my first corporate job. I wasn't the leader of the group, much less the preacher. So I did what any other person would do when put on the spot. I opened my Bible to a random psalm and started reading.

> They have left me among the dead,
>   and I lie like a corpse in a grave.
> I am forgotten,
>   cut off from your care.
> You have thrown me into the lowest pit,
>   into the darkest depths.
> Your anger weighs me down;
>   with wave after wave you have engulfed me.
>
> You have driven my friends away
>   by making me repulsive to them.
> I am in a trap with no way of escape.

As the words of Psalm 88:5-8 began to register, I cringed. This was not the most encouraging passage I could have chosen for the moment. But I kept reading because I didn't know what else to do.

Then our new friend interrupted me.

"That's what I need! I need Jesus!"

I looked at the passage again. *Where does it say anything about Jesus?* Well, he was there, even if not explicitly mentioned.

Our little men's group shared the gospel with the man and he was accepted into God's Kingdom.

Our men's group didn't need a fancy vision statement to know what to do. The car didn't swerve into the parking lot because of an eye-catching church logo or a compelling slogan on the sign. What God made clear was our true purpose: Share Jesus with the person right in front of you.

This next part of the checklist helps to answer an important question: *What can you do to shift your church to an outward focus?* Without a rekindling of evangelism and outreach, a struggling church will not be revitalized.

A Dangerous Stillness and the Conversion Ratio

More than half of current churchgoers do not share their faith with others.[1] The church is sitting still and becoming apathetic. This apathy means fewer people are hearing the gospel. It's time to move outward again. In chapter 1, I gave details about the erosion of evangelism among churches in North America. Even among growing churches, evangelism is often absent. In this chapter, I will present some solutions to the lack of evangelism. First, it's helpful to diagnose the degree of the problem in your church.

One way of determining evangelistic health is through a metric called *conversion ratio*. This ratio tells you how many people in your church it takes to win one person for Christ. A healthy church will have a conversion ratio of 20:1 or less. The smaller the conversion ratio, the fewer people it takes in your church to reach others. For example, a conversion ratio of 1:1 means each person in your church is reaching one person for Christ each year. A conversion ratio of 100:1 means that for every one hundred people in your church, only one person is reached for Christ per year. You can calculate the conversion ratio with a simple formula: average weekly attendance for the year divided by number of conversions in the same year.[2]

If a church averages three hundred in weekly attendance and sees twenty people come to Christ in a year, their conversion ratio is 15:1. Take a moment and calculate your church's conversion ratio and compare it to the following conversion health scale.

20:1 or less: *Healthy.* Your church is sharing the gospel regularly.

21:1 to 50:1: *Somewhat healthy.* A core group of people are sharing the gospel.

51:1 to 80:1: *Somewhat unhealthy.* A few people are sharing the gospel, but not many.

81:1 or more: *Unhealthy.* Your church is not sharing the gospel with others.

Sadly, most churches in North America are unhealthy. In fact, the average conversion ratio among churches in the United States is 85:1. Less than four percent of churches meet the criteria for being healthy. There is a dangerous lack of evangelistic activity. It's time to stir these stagnant waters.

The Big Invite

The return to an outward focus begins with a simple invite. One of the best ways to rekindle an outward focus is by encouraging a few of your willing people to invite their neighbors to church. A smattering of guests every week can be the kick start your church needs.

I call it "the big invite," but it can start small—with you. The only way your church has *no one* inviting others is if *you* are not inviting others. Even if nobody else will bring their neighbors to church, you can. Every pastor and church leader should be able to bring one guest a month to church. If you can get a small group in your church to join you, perhaps ten other people, you will soon have a regular stream of guests. These guests often come attached to families. If each invitation produces two guests on average, and you have ten people accomplishing one invitation a month, you will have 240 guests in a year.

Evangelism is more about having an inviting culture than it is about hosting events. Successful evangelistic events often get a lot of press. Rightly so. But the most successful churches have a culture of evangelism. An event has a start-and-end date. Often after an event, people move back into previous patterns. But when evangelism is built into the culture of the church, it has no end date. The culture supports evangelism as an ongoing pattern.

Evangelistic programs with one key distinctive can be a helpful tool in building an evangelistic culture. Such programs are helpful *if you share success stories*. What gets measured gets done, and you become what you celebrate.

Twenty or thirty years ago, many churches canceled their evangelism programs due to waning interest. What had once drawn dozens of participants dwindled to only a handful. When the handful gave up, outreach died altogether. Part of the problem was that churches pushed evangelism as an expectation of *duty* rather than the excitement of celebration. Some programs worked better than others, but every evangelism program will work better if people are drawn by the excitement of celebration and not driven by the guilt of duty. Evangelism success stories should be shared through as many church communication channels as possible, including the platform on Sunday morning.

The lead pastor must set the example. Rather than explaining evangelistic methods, *show* what evangelism looks like in your own life. Start by inviting people to church. An invitation to church is not evangelism, but it will lead to gospel-sharing opportunities. When pastors and church leaders invite others, the culture of a big invite begins to take hold among the congregation.

As a leader, free up one to three hours a week on your calendar with the explicit purpose of inviting guests and sharing your faith. What you schedule is what you will do. Make the time and stick to it. Your church will follow if you will lead.

Group connection is the glue. Not only should you invite people to a worship experience, but you should also connect them to a group setting. Our research shows that people are five times more likely to stay in a church after five years if they get connected to a group. The group setting—whatever the structure—is the place where deep gospel conversations occur. Most sermons do not have a Q&A attached to them, but most groups allow for participants to ask questions. The worship experience is often the front door, the place where new people first connect. For this reason, the gospel must be shared from the platform and pulpit. But where the gospel takes root is in the relational setting of groups.

Right around the Corner but off the Radar

The story of the American church is one of small, established congregations. Most American churches have fewer than one hundred people and have been meeting for several decades. And most of these churches are located in residential neighborhoods. They are exactly where God wants them, at least in terms of their location. The problem is that a significant number of neighborhood churches have forgotten why they exist. They are right around the corner but off the radar of their neighbors.

A few months after being called to my current church, I had an epiphany about our purpose. On this particular Sunday morning, we were maxing out the parking lot and people were getting a little too creative in finding a spot. One elderly couple left their Buick LeSabre on the front steps. Our church campus is just over four acres, in a neighborhood with absolutely no room to expand, and our parking lot is simply too small.

We already had four services on Sunday—three in English and one in Spanish—and our problem wasn't space inside the building. Plenty of seats remained available in our worship services, and we still had a few rooms in our facility for on-campus groups to grow. We just couldn't park people.

Relocation was not an option. We are essentially on the west coast of Florida and land is not available. Some had joked about building a parking garage, but the structure would cost somewhere between $20,000 and $40,000 a spot. We could buy every family in the church an SUV for less. Adding more services was still an option, but there is a point of diminishing returns with multiple services.

At home that evening, I stared at a Google Maps image of our church, scouring every street for potential parking. Nothing. When I zoomed out of the image, all I saw was grid after grid of neighborhoods. Then I noticed something else. Several other churches were buried in neighborhoods just like us. I knew that many of them were struggling. Their two- and three-acre parking lots were mostly empty on Sundays.

But then I quickly realized that God had placed those churches there. He had given them their buildings and parking lots. Looking at the digital map of my community convicted me. God wanted those churches to thrive in their neighborhoods. The goal is Kingdom growth, not church growth.

Our leaders spent the next several months working through a plan to maximize the use of our campus. With a reconfigured parking lot, we determined we could grow by a couple hundred more people. But we will never be a megachurch. In fact, the vast majority of my church members have no desire to be a megachurch. We will always be a neighborhood church. And we agreed that the ultimate goal is to *send people out*. Rather than trying to gather as many people as we can onto our own campus (church growth), we committed ourselves to help revitalize as many churches as we can in our area (Kingdom growth). Some might be skeptical. I understand. Most neighborhood churches had their heyday decades ago. But I'm hopeful. You should be hopeful too. Perhaps you are leading a neighborhood church. Maybe you attend a neighborhood church. Let me encourage you with these words: You are *not* the past. You are the future.

What Is a Neighborhood Church?

In simplest terms, a neighborhood church is one surrounded by residences. An exact definition of a neighborhood does not exist, partly because they exist in various forms. Chicago, for example, has an extensive network of neighborhoods, each with its own identity and personality. But neighborhoods are not limited to big cities. The suburbs have subdivisions, which can act as neighborhoods. Small towns have neighborhood enclaves as well. Therefore, the neighborhood church is found in urban areas, suburban areas, and in small towns.

The neighborhood is a local community with a specific identity that is set within a larger city, small town, or suburb. It is both geographic and social. A neighborhood is geographic in the sense that it has well-defined boundaries, sometimes determined by a city council or other government agency. But it is social in that the people of the community will identify with a particular neighborhood.

For example, I went to high school in Louisville, Kentucky. My family lived in the St. Matthews neighborhood. I'm sure there is an official boundary to St. Matthews, but we didn't need it. We knew when we weren't in our neighborhood anymore. To this day, I often specify that I lived in St. Matthews when I mention my time in Louisville.

The neighborhood church is a congregation associated with a particular neighborhood. Unfortunately, many neighborhood churches have not fared well in recent decades. Neighborhood churches were originally started *in* a community and *for* the community.[3] At times, a neighborhood church will carry the same name as the community. Neighborhood churches can be from any denominational background (or none at all). They should draw people from the surrounding area, but many have suffered from white flight. In most cases, neighborhood churches are not located directly on a major road, but rather are situated on secondary roads. Neighborhood church locations are built into the fabric of the community, and most of them are landlocked by surrounding homes.

Neighborhood churches are typically smaller and more established. They can be larger (several hundred, or in rare cases larger), but most are close to the median church size of seventy-five weekly attenders. Most neighborhood churches are also well established. They have been in the community for quite some time. The median church age is ninety-four years.[4] Many neighborhood churches have been in the same location for decades.

Typically, you can recognize a neighborhood church when you see it. A rural church on a state road is not a neighborhood church. A megachurch right off the interstate may do a lot of good in the region, but it's not a neighborhood church. Neighborhood churches are in every city and small town. They are numerous, perhaps the largest single category of churches. Their location—including your location—is not an accident. The nation needs a movement of healthy neighborhood churches. God placed you right where he wants you. Now it's time to do something about it. Fair warning: This movement will mean a lot of messy churches.

Why Healthy Churches Are Messy

"They aren't a real church. Most of the people there are immature."

I nodded without a smile. The person making the comment was a member of my church. The church he referenced was a large, growing church down the road. I wasn't sure whether I agreed with him or not. His comment floated by without much acknowledgment one way or the other.

Several years later, the remark still sticks with me. Given all the interactions I have with people, it's surprising I even remember it. But I know why it stuck with me. God wanted to teach me something. The church in question was certainly a real church, but it was true that most of their people were immature in their faith. The church was a mess, but they were healthy.

Unhealthy Messy Churches

First, I want to get an obvious point out of the way: Some churches are messy because they are unhealthy. When congregants elevate personal preferences over the gospel, it creates a mess. When church leaders make pragmatic growth the goal instead of the glory of God, it creates a mess. Plenty of unhealthy messy churches exist—large and small. But there is a healthy kind of messy church—one that is growing by conversion, not transfer.

Healthy Messy Churches

Some churches are messy precisely because they are healthy. When a church is growing and new people are coming in for discipleship, it's hard to keep things neat and tidy. Allow me to present a hypothetical case.

If a church has a 1:1 conversion ratio for three years—that is, on average, everyone in the church reaches one person for Christ every year, the church will double in size each year. If the church started with one hundred people, it will have eight hundred people attending after three years. That fact alone will create some stresses and strains for the congregation and its leadership.

Now assume that the one hundred members at the beginning were mature believers. This church now has seven hundred relatively new believers. After three amazing years of evangelism, less than 13 percent of the church would be considered mature in the faith. A cynic might make a case for describing such a church as dysfunctional—and it might seem that way on the surface. But any church that approaches that level of sustained outreach and assimilation is, in reality, a model of health.

Healthy churches are inevitably messy. How should you lead them?

How to Lead a Healthy Messy Church

From a high-level perspective, three areas are universal in helping a healthy messy church grow well. Every church that wants to become healthier should emphasize these three things.

1. *New Member Class.* A new member class is crucial, whether your church is fast-growing or slow-growing. But messy, fast-growing churches especially need a way to connect with and assimilate a lot of new people. Are they new believers? Are they transferring from other churches? How did they decide to come to your church? How can they get connected to more than the worship service? A new member class helps answer many of these important questions.

2. *Clear Doctrine and High Expectations.* Along with an influx of new people comes the responsibility of being open and honest about the doctrine and expectations

of the church. I fear for some fast-growing churches who downplay doctrine—or worse, hide it—when assimilating new people. Downplaying your doctrine creates a culture in which people will leave as quickly as they come. Additionally, healthy churches are upfront about expectations for church members. A fast-growing, high-expectations church is a church primed for gospel fruit.

3. *A Process of Discipleship.* A new member class helps answer important questions on the front end. Clear doctrine and high expectations let people know where you and they stand. But people will not grow in their faith and maturity without a process of discipleship. Discipleship involves the pathways people take to grow in Christ. At most churches, this includes worship attendance, group involvement, giving, and serving. A process of discipleship details the way in which people engage in these areas to become more mature believers.

Healthy churches are messy. It's easy to look in from the outside and say, "Half that church is immature!" But such disdain may be misguided. While a state of perpetual immaturity is a recipe for disaster, a steady influx of immature believers being discipled is exactly what we should desire and pursue. After all, discipleship is what Jesus commanded us to do.[5]

9

Pathway

The Realistic Next Step

THE BLEEDING EDGE is never polished. Blazing a trail requires a machete, not a scalpel. The most polished and largest churches often receive praise for being the most creative. Certainly some of these churches are creative. But many of them grew by perfecting the innovations of others rather than creating something new of their own. I don't fault any church for refining existing ideas, but that process is more science than art, more engineering than creativity.

During the pandemic of 2020, one of the more stressful decisions involved reopening church campuses for in-person gatherings and worship services. Church leaders faced a no-win scenario of when and how to restart. Some of the largest churches struggled the most—for obvious reasons. They had to consider a greater number of people with a broader spectrum of opinions.

The smaller, more nimble churches in our area were the ones who led the way with creative reopening strategies. I remember brainstorming with my team about how to approach reopening our campus. One staff member asked about two megachurches in our region and what they planned to do.

"They have not decided and plan to remain closed indefinitely," someone replied.

"Why?"

"They don't want to reopen until they can go back to the way they were doing things before the pandemic."

I realized something. These two megachurches, known for their modern ministry approaches, had become today's version of a stuck traditional church. They seemingly had given up on creative solutions in favor of returning to *the way we've always done things*. For years, every church in our area felt like they were playing catch-up to these churches. Now the roles were reversed, and few people seemed to realize it.

When optimism and creativity come together, a pathway opens up to a brighter future. Optimism is the belief in God's promise of greater things. Creativity is the process of putting the belief into action. Blazing a new pathway is exciting.

But what is the most realistic next step?

A helpful tool is a strategy called the MHAG. It is one of the best ways to determine your realistic next step in revitalization.

Creating an MHAG

MHAG (pronounced *em-hag*) stands for *mid holy audacious goal*.[1] The key to a good MHAG is choosing an initiative or emphasis that lasts months, not years. The best strategies to spark creativity often come with mid-length timelines. Thus the first word, *mid*. About six months is often ideal. Most churches will tire of a continual emphasis that lasts much longer. Additionally, most churches are not able to handle multiple emphases at the same time. The focus on one mid-length goal keeps the congregation aligned and engaged.

The second term, *holy*, establishes that the aim of the goal is to give God glory. Any creative effort must begin with prayer. Untethered creativity will inevitably float away from a Christ-centered focus. The age-old adage is true: No one drifts toward holiness. Our sin nature nudges us toward compromise and disobedience.[2] Compromised creativity becomes either rank pragmatism or undisciplined spirituality. In the name of creativity, some churches sacrifice what is holy for what works. Other churches sacrifice spiritual disciplines.

The third term, *audacious*, means the goal must be bold. It must get the attention of your church. For example, we worked with one church that had a goal of meeting every neighbor within several blocks of the church. For six months, the church created an outreach effort involving many members. They brought gifts. They wrote letters. Each month for six months, every neighbor received some form of contact from the church. Nothing was asked of these neighbors other than soliciting prayer requests. After six months, the neighborhood's perception of the church had moved from apathetic to positive.

The last term, *goal*, refers to the singular focus of the MHAG. When my team consults with established churches that are struggling, we often narrow our recommendations to one next step. In many churches, the idea of doing several strategies at once is simply unattainable. As mentioned in chapter 4, no doctor would attempt ten surgeries on a patient all at the same time, even if the patient claimed to be ready. Few churches are able to accomplish more than one MHAG at a time.

Momentum builds over the course of several successful MHAGs. Each successive six-month initiative acts like a wave pushing the church in a healthier direction. A successful MHAG has the potential to be one of the best pathways for revitalizing your church. But how do you implement a successful one?

Write the MHAG

This step begins with you. Take into consideration what excites your church. If possible, build an MHAG around something people already believe will work. Here are two examples to help you write out your own MHAG.

- In the next [time frame], we will [some sort of action with a concrete measurement] in hopes that [measurable number] people will [something you want people to do or attend].

- By [give an exact end date], our [name of church or ministry area] will [some sort of action] that will reach [measurable number] people for [name your expressed purpose].

When you fill in the brackets, you will get something like this example: *In the next six months, our church will pray for and leave door hangers on 2,000 homes in our community.*

Writing the MHAG is a critical step. Make sure you include a specific action with a measurable outcome. Write your MHAG on a whiteboard in your office, or another prominent place, as a continual reminder to stay focused on the goal.

Find Your Champions

Successful MHAGs always involve other leaders. No pastor should try to lead a churchwide initiative without the help of others. Frankly, you cannot blaze a new trail alone. If you want to create new pathways in the church, other leaders must be a part of the process. Perhaps you have leaders in mind who could jump in immediately. More likely, you have a small pool of potential candidates. Good leaders are hard to find, are often spread thin, and are already involved in other areas of the church. What can you do to equip new leaders and delegate to them? Some simple guidelines will help you delegate while also empowering your MHAG champions.

Start by identifying leaders with two simple questions. First, who has influence in the church? Second, who is supportive of leadership? MHAGs don't necessarily require the most competent leaders, but audacious goals require both influence and support. People who are both influential and supportive often make great MHAG champions.

Once you find your champions, they must be equipped. Don't make the mistake of delegating without equipping. Remember, you're blazing a trail with this new pathway—heading toward new places previously unknown. You need people who know how to use a machete more than a scalpel. MHAGs don't have to be polished works of perfection. You simply need people who will get the task done. Walk your leaders through these four steps:

Show: You may have to do the first MHAG while others watch and learn. Do the work while they observe, ask questions, and begin to contribute.

Explain: While you are showing your champions the work, consistently reinforce *why* you are undertaking the MHAG. The whole point is to create a new pathway for the church to improve the health of the body. Though MHAGs include tasks, the greater purpose is to build momentum.

Ask: After your champions have seen you do a few tasks, ask them to start contributing while you observe. While you watch, ask them questions such as, "What are you learning? How do you believe this goal will affect our church? How can this goal help our church become healthier?" These questions will help establish the importance of the MHAG.

Support: Even after you have completely delegated tasks, make sure you are available to your leaders to answer their questions and respond to their concerns. Likely, you have encountered people who are resistant to change. These influencers showed you support when you led, and you will need to do the same for them as they lead.[3]

Set Your Timetables

After selecting your group of leaders, the next step is to set deadlines. Timetables are mutually agreed-upon intervals in which to accomplish the MHAG. They include individual deadlines that move the process toward the goal. I recommend timetables no shorter than six months and no longer than twelve months. Let's assume you want to accomplish the example mentioned above: *In the next six months, our church will pray for and leave door hangers on 2,000 homes in our community.* What are some ways to set timetables? You can begin by breaking down this large goal into six smaller goals.

Month 1: Identify 2,000 homes and create a system for sending people to them.

Month 2: Design and develop the door hangers telling the residents they have been prayed for. Include a way for people to contact the church and invite them to mention their prayer requests.

Month 3: Recruit volunteers and train them.

Month 4: Implement the effort and complete the prayer initiative.

Month 5: Follow up with those who contact the church about prayer requests.

Month 6: Celebrate the success of the effort with the entire church through worship services, social media, newsletters, and other methods of communication.

After completing the MHAG, make sure to meet with your leadership team to debrief. Document areas of improvement and the parts that went well. This document will be helpful should you do the effort again, and it will also help as you launch the next MHAG.

Use Lead Measures, Not Lag Measures

As you set each MHAG, consider using lead goals rather than lag goals. When you set a growth goal of 20 percent, it's a lag measure because the growth occurs after the effort. The lead goal is the effort made to accomplish the lag goal. Here's an example: I want this ministry to grow by twenty-four people over six months (lag measure), so I will contact ten new people each month, hoping to gain four of them (lead measure). MHAGs work because they involve lead measures rather than lag measures.

Remind People Regularly with Inspiration

Brutal honesty is necessary when identifying the signs of a dying church. Slow erosion of attendance, short pastor tenures, obsession over facilities, and focusing on glories of the past are just a few of the problems in dying churches. Members tend to be selfish and have a high resistance to change. Criticism becomes rampant when the comfort of the status quo is challenged.

The point of an MHAG is to break the church free from this death spiral. The most fruitful MHAGs follow an awakening of church members, but an MHAG can also be a wake-up call. If you're going to blaze a new trail, it can't be done with pessimism and negativity. New pathways form through creative optimism. Leadership is a process in which ordinary people bring forth the best in themselves and others. Inspiration is crucial to help followers embrace a shared vision.[4]

Regular reminders of the MHAG can come through various means of communication. Lead pastors can preach a sermon series that encompasses the overarching themes of the MHAG. Enlist your children's ministry and your student ministry to help with part of the MHAG. As the MHAG progresses, use social media and church newsletters to celebrate the completion of certain tasks.

Remember, you become what you celebrate. When church leaders celebrate negativity, the culture of the church moves toward pessimism. In extreme cases, negativity breeds bitterness, skepticism, or even hatred. Godly inspiration never comes through pessimism. Check the tone of your social media posts and sermons. Do not act dismissively with church members or trash-talk your community. Optimism is what inspires.

Create a System of Accountability

Optimism detached from accountability results in fleeting inspiration. Accountability without optimism produces grudging compliance. When optimism is coupled with accountability, people will work toward a goal with a sense of purpose and encouragement. Let's look again at the previously mentioned goal: *In the next six months, our church will pray for and leave door hangers on 2,000 homes in our community.* How can you create a system of accountability for this MHAG?

Each month's progress goal should have a deadline and a team member responsible for its completion. Maintain regular communication with your team leaders. Team leaders should maintain regular communication with their volunteers. The system of accountability could be something as simple as text reminders on the front end and email follow-up on the back end. Accountability should be helpful and encouraging, not overbearing. Are the leaders finding enough volunteers to reach 2,000 homes? Is the design for the door hangers coming in on time? At the beginning of each month, send a reminder to the leader in charge. Halfway through each month, check in and make sure the leaders have what they need to accomplish the goal. At the end of the month, thank everyone for their work. Above all, maintain a positive posture with your communication.

The 100 Factor of Negativity

Nothing will derail momentum like negativity. Overblown drama can distract people from the task at hand. Gossip can magnify discord and pain. One or two toxic people can contaminate dozens of others. Every negative word has the power of one hundred positive words.[5] Think of encouragement and discouragement as weights on opposite sides of a scale. One piece of discouragement weighs the same as one hundred pieces of encouragement. In your marriage, your family, your work relationships, and the church, the 100 factor of negativity is always in effect. If you are consistently negative, you are digging a deep, dark hole. Negativity has many variants, all of which can quickly halt progress on the new pathway you are trying to create. If you're blazing a trail into new areas, think of negativity as a highly contagious virus, infecting your entire team and causing an immediate halt to all progress.

You must protect your MHAG from negativity. The other side of tomorrow includes a more positive, brighter future for your church. But you can't get there via pessimism. The final chapter includes a case study on how to put all seven principles into action. It's time to start blazing a trail and creating a pathway to better church health.

10

Completing Your Church
Revitalization Checklist

You ARE NOT THE HERO of your church. Christ is. Any revitalization effort detached from the centrality of Jesus will ultimately fail. God alone determines whether dry bones live, but he may ask you, like Ezekiel, to speak a prophetic message that starts the rattle.[1]

Pastor Ryan inherited a mess when he was called to a bedroom community in Ohio. His church had been through four splits in ten years. The last split occurred when the previous lead pastor walked out of a raucous business meeting. Nobody saw him leave. Nobody ever saw him again.

The business meeting had taken a wrong turn when the

moderator asked for any new business. One family took the opportunity to accuse another family of stealing one of the church's Christmas trees. Someone blurted out, "Nobody would steal one of those trees. They're ugly." Then the family that had donated the trees got angry and started making accusations about people who were stealing from the church by using the copy machine for personal use. After the yelling stopped, a motion was made to investigate the copier servicing agreement.

When Ryan arrived for his first day, the church secretary warned him, "Don't ask about the copier or Christmas trees." He had no idea why, but the look on her face was enough reason to avoid those topics.

At his first deacons meeting, Ryan learned that the issues were deeper than unnecessary spats between families. Apparently, one deacon had recently been accused of threatening his boss with a firearm. His elderly mother had filed for a restraining order against her son. The deacons wanted to know Ryan's thoughts on the matter.

The church had declined from 400 to 120 in average attendance, but giving had recently stabilized and young families were starting to visit, not knowing the church's history. The church's location was a draw for people. New subdivisions had begun encroaching on old farmland. At the time, Ryan was twenty-eight years old, married for three years, and his wife was pregnant with their second child. After five years of bi-vocational ministry, this church was his first full-time pastoral role. He was a respected master mechanic, a profession he loved and had done since he was sixteen. Though Ryan loved to fix things and get them running smoothly, this church presented new challenges.

How might a revitalization checklist help someone like Ryan?

Three "Knows" of Church Revitalization

Before jumping into the checklist, Ryan knew he needed a better understanding of the situation. By mastering three "knows," Ryan would develop a broader knowledge base for working through the checklist. The three knows are simple: *know yourself*, *know your church*, and *know your community*.

1. Know Yourself

Self-awareness is one of the key intangibles of leadership. Many pastors die by a thousand paper cuts, and these cuts are often inflicted by unforced errors resulting from a lack of self-awareness. Ryan remembered one of his annual reviews from his days as a mechanic. His boss told him, "You're smarter than any other mechanic, but you can't use your intellect to make customers feel like they don't know anything."

Ryan realized he had a tendency to use his intellect as a weapon. This realization was a critical lesson. Leaders should never act condescendingly toward those they lead. Knowledge is not a weapon to be brandished, but rather a resource to be shared.

Leaders become self-aware by inviting confidants to call out their foibles and mistakes. The best lessons in self-awareness happen in the moment—when you're caught in the act, so to speak, and can more easily be shown how you're coming across. Ask a trusted friend or colleague to pull you aside when needed. Give him or her the freedom to tell you privately when you are devolving into behavior that is detrimental. Everyone has blind spots. Self-aware leaders invite trusted advisors to point out their blind spots.

2. Know Your Church

Truly knowing your church takes time. Often, it's time pastors don't have, especially in church revitalization efforts. Church health surveys can help with uncovering major problems,[2] but revitalization work requires more than one churchwide survey. Pastor Ryan got creative. He researched old articles from the local paper and read every report about the church. Thankfully, they were all positive. Most of the drama was contained within the church and the community knew little about it. Then he dug into the minutes of every business meeting. They read like a soap opera, and certain names surfaced again and again. Ryan also asked the secretary to find every old church newsletter that was still available. As he perused these documents, the dots connected in his mind. He correlated attendance patterns with newsletter blurbs about community outreach and newspaper articles about community involvement. The conclusion was simple and obvious: The church grew when reaching outward and declined when focused inward. Ryan now had hard evidence, and he created a presentation to share with the other leaders in the church.

3. Know Your Community

After examining the demographics of the community, Ryan identified a disconnect between the people of the church and their neighbors.[3] The fastest growing segment of the population were millennials and their children, which explained why most visitors were younger. The church had a large segment of the older congregants, but also several young families. The problem was that all the programs and the budget resources were targeted to the older generations.

Not only was the community getting younger, but there was also an influx of ethnic minorities. Bilingual Latinos comprised 30 percent of the community, and almost all were younger and middle-class. This was a surprise to those who remembered the days of a slow-moving farming community. Ryan began crafting a plan to reach outward into the neighborhood. The story of Ryan's church is one I hear over and over. The two demographics most often overlooked are the prevalence of young people and ethnic minorities.

Seven Steps of Church Revitalization

Every church has different issues. The remainder of the chapter will be a case study that follows Ryan through the seven points of revitalization. There is no way one book can cover every component of revitalization, but the seven points here will help shift the culture of your church.

The checklist exists to demonstrate visual progress, constant accountability, and consistent focus. It is meant to be more cultural and less comprehensive. The approach is collaborative, not formulaic. One person cannot lead the effort; it takes a group of leaders. The checklist is flexible, not systematized. It's meant to work with whatever systems or polity are already in place at your church. The checklist is practical, not theological. My goal is to help you connect your convictions to the heart of your people in a way they understand.

1. Establishing the Right Priority

Ryan took the demographic report to the next church council meeting. After completing the Discerning the Drivers of Decline exercise (see chapter 3), he knew the major problems were an overly nostalgic church focused too much on traditions and personal preferences. Rather than harp on the problems, he decided to propose a solution to the council. The changing demographics of the community were his entrée.

He asked the group of eight, "What is the largest generation in our community?"

Everyone responded, "Boomers or builders." They were shocked when Ryan told them millennials were the largest generation, and the second largest generation was their children, Gen Z.

"I see it in the grocery store," Margaret spoke up. Everyone paused and looked at her. The soft-spoken matriarch was the most trusted person in the church, and after seventy years as a member, also the longest tenured. "There are more young people in this community than ever before. I don't know how to reach them, but our church will not last another generation if we don't try."

It was the moment that changed the course of the church. Nostalgia was still a problem, especially with entrenched and dated programs. People still elevated their music preferences. But a renewed devotion to reaching younger people surfaced. Ryan captured the beginnings of momentum. After years of sitting dormant, the flywheel was starting to turn.

Ryan told his council, "The priority is not necessarily to *grow big*, but rather to *go out*. God will provide the growth, but we must be obedient to his commission."

They were listening and willing to move.

2. Setting the Right Pace

A few leaders started talking about the church's potential to reach the community, but Ryan was discerning enough to know they could not move too quickly. He worked through the Pace Acceptance Matrix (chapter 4) and realized that well over half the congregation fell into the high-resistance category. He was new to the church and understood that the pace of change would have to be more gradual than urgent. Additionally, with stable giving and attendance, he knew he had time to implement his plan.

Prayer was Ryan's starting point, and he combined a prayer effort with his neighborhood outreach plan.[4] The church started a prayer-walk initiative and used door hangers to ask the neighbors for prayer requests. Within a couple of days, the church was able to follow up with more than twenty families and pray about their needs. Two families visited the church within a month.

Ryan knew this one effort would not be enough, so he became more intentional about his own personal evangelism. He set aside five hours a week to reach outward into the community. Both he and his wife invited neighbors over for dinner. Ryan began to interact more with people in the local coffee shop, at the bank, and at high school football games. He viewed his role as not only pastoring the people in his church but also pastoring the people in the community.

The pace was slower than Ryan would have preferred, but he intentionally did not make the change effort feel like a crisis. Though some churches need immediate intervention, others—where giving and attendance patterns are stable—are better served through gradual change efforts. A crisis may enable faster change, but quick change may or may not settle into the culture. Gradual change is more likely to create cultural shifts that benefit the church in the long run.

3. Determining the Right Perspective

After a few weeks, more young families started attending. But the older generation was also drawn to the church. Ryan underestimated how much the older generation appreciated the focus on the next generation. The church had grown from an average attendance of 120 to 160. It's at this point that managing expectations becomes crucial. Churches like growth until it starts messing with the power structure.

When enough new people start coming to shift the balance of power, the church's perspective of growth changes.

Ryan got in front of these expectations. He told his church, "As we grow, this new group will not be exactly like us, and that's okay."

He also had to deal with discouragement in his own soul. Growth was occurring but not as quickly as he wanted. The church had a great location, but the older group in the church could only do so much. They were short on volunteers, and a couple of new families commented that the children's programming was not quite like the larger church down the road.

To keep the right perspective, Ryan asked three deacons to encourage him through accountability. He gave them permission to point out the times he was moving too quickly or acting from a place of urgency or disappointment. When the pastor does not have the right perspective, the church will struggle to move in the right direction.

4. Managing the Right People

As the flywheel began to move more quickly, Ryan couldn't help but think about how much more needed to be done. He made the decision to love the people he had rather than dream about the people he wished he had. Pastors must love their churches the way they are right now, not some future version. The change in Ryan's heart became evident in the way he led. He was more relaxed in his leadership and more likable as a person.

When he worked through the Capacity Formula (chapter 6), the results were surprising. His church scored 20 percent, which is on the border between average capacity and above average capacity. Ryan realized he had more support than he'd previously thought. He had been neglecting his supporters and focusing on the malcontents, who were taking up too much time. He shifted his focus to a new personal leadership strategy: flip the amount of time spent on malcontents and supporters. He would not ignore those who had issues with him, but they would no longer get the majority of his time.

5. Fixing the Right Place

Most guests mentioned the cleanliness of the facility, and everyone loved the location. After doing the Church Facility Assessment (chapter 7), he noted their score was on the high side of acceptable. But one sore spot was quite evident: the bathrooms. They had not been updated since the campus was built.

When one of his grumpier members started complaining about the move away from a specific children's program, Ryan's first thought was, *You have never volunteered in the children's ministry. What do you care?* But rather than push back on the grump, Ryan redirected the man's energy into one of his strengths.

"Would you be open to helping lead an effort to renovate our bathrooms?"

"Can I add an extra urinal in the men's room and change toilet paper suppliers?"

"Deal. Just make sure there is a way for kids to reach the sink to wash their hands."

"Thanks, pastor. I'll get it done the right way."

In a single conversation, Ryan was able to address a major facility issue and win over another supporter. The grump never again complained about children's programming. Even better, he volunteered to clean the bathrooms every week to ensure his work remained pristine. The bathrooms sparkled to the glory of God.

6. Rekindling the Right Purpose

A few months passed, and the church began to pick up more momentum. The community started talking about the church, and Ryan was a recognizable presence, especially at high school football games. The coach asked him to be the team's chaplain and give words of encouragement before each home game.

Despite the positive movement, Ryan knew something was still missing. He calculated their conversion ratio (chapter 8) and realized they were not seeing as many people come to Christ as they should. Their 70:1 ratio was somewhat unhealthy. The bathrooms may have been clean, but the church was not messy enough. Many of their new people were already believers. They had moved to the community because it was becoming a desirable place to live, with affordable housing.

Ryan tweaked the curriculum for the new members class to include an emphasis on inviting friends, coworkers, and family members who were not believers. With the cultural shifts already occurring in the church, the new emphasis was well received. In his sermons, Ryan began mentioning success stories of church members sharing their faith. He took to heart the idea that the church becomes what the people celebrate. By celebrating those who shared Jesus and accepted Jesus, the true purpose of the church was rekindled.

7. Finding the Right Pathway

Though some in the church still complained regularly about any number of frivolous items, Ryan could feel the gathering momentum and knew they were on the right path. He worked with the council on developing a six-month MHAG (chapter 9), and the council members believed it would help get the flywheel moving even more rapidly.

Their MHAG was simple: Over the next six months, have as many as half the members invite one new family to church. The council divided up the membership of the church and spent the first sixty days challenging the members to invite someone to church. They met their goal of getting half the congregation to commit to the MHAG. Every week, Ryan mentioned the effort and incorporated success stories into his sermons. The council sent out text and email reminders to everyone in the effort. By the end of six months, two dozen new families had visited the church and Ryan had received his first phone call from the denominational office.

"We hear what's happening at your church. Could you speak at our annual meeting about what God is doing?"

Ryan wanted to tell the denominational executive that he had just gotten off the phone with an elderly member who threatened to leave the church because her classroom was too cold. But he didn't. He humbly accepted the invitation, then went to check on the southside door that kept jamming.

An Unglamorous Calling for the Glory of God

Ministry isn't glamorous. And the moment that ministry does become glamorous, you become an anti-minister. Church revitalization is gritty work, but God is glorified in the impossible challenge of leading a church back to health.

The church's biggest problem is not a lack of giving, a lack of people, or a lack of leadership. The church's biggest problem is the lack of assurance in the pursuit of God's glory. Slow giving trends are a symptom of a greater problem. So are poor leadership and a decline in average worship attendance. The solution to the church's problem is a tireless pursuit of God's glory.

Glory implies weight, something substantial or lasting. To glory in something is to show it is central and most important. Nothing should equal the weight of God in your life. Every great leader dies. Ethics deteriorate. Economies putter out. The best buildings crumble. The best schools phase in and out. The biggest churches come and go. Only the glory of God carries with it the weight of blessed assurance.

We don't just recruit people to come to church on the

weekend. We compel people to become active participants in the greatest mission this world has ever known—the proclamation of the glory of God to the ends of the earth. Why do we exist? The only way it matters is if our life's mission is bringing glory to God.

The prophet Isaiah records clear words from God about his people: "I have made them for my glory. It was I who created them."[5] You were *made* for this. Made to be saved. Redeemed to be sent. Sent for the glory of God. Dig into the grit of ministry and find God's glory. Rely on the Holy Spirit over personal charm. Depend on prayer over strategy. Give up self-reliance and become powerless for the name of Christ. You may never be recognized for your work. You may go decades before someone thanks you for your ministry.

We need more unglamorous pastors like Ambrose Gilbert Sapp, my wife's grandfather. He toiled in obscurity among the rolling fields of Kentucky farms, shepherding in poverty without any glory or recognition. He preached the gospel until he died, and the next pastor took his place. Give us more faithful servants like Ambrose Sapp. There's no way to know with certainty, but I believe thousands—including my wife—are in God's Kingdom because of his faithfulness.

If God can save any person, then he can save any church. Yours included. The pursuit of God's glory will take you to the other side of tomorrow. Onward.

Notes

**INTRODUCTION: LEADING YOUR CHURCH INTO AN ERA OF
RENEWED OPTIMISM**

1. Romans 15:13.
2. Portions of this section were adapted from Sam Rainer, "Your Church Is
   Worth the Effort," *Leading the Established Church* (blog), July 12, 2015,
   https://samrainer.com/2015/07/your-church-is-worth-the-effort/.
3. Psalm 22:1-2, 9-10, 22-23, 25.
4. Job 5:16.
5. Edward Mote, "My Hope Is Built on Nothing Less," 1834. Public domain.
6. Check us out at ChurchAnswers.com.
7. See Yvonna S. Lincoln and Egon G. Guba, *Naturalistic Inquiry* (Newbury
   Park, CA: Sage Publications, 1985).
8. Aaron Earls, "The Church Growth Gap: The Big Get Bigger While
   the Small Get Smaller," *Christianity Today*, March 6, 2019, https://
   www.christianitytoday.com/news/2019/march/lifeway-research-church
   -growth-attendance-size.html.
9. See Mark Clifton (@johnmarkclifton), "It's not a small church. It's a
   normative size church. Churches w/less than 100 in worship are 63%
   of all SBC Churches," Twitter, July 21, 2016, 8:00 p.m., https://twitter
   .com/johnmarkclifton/status/756292770004803585. The term *normative*
   typically refers to a value judgment. Perhaps some churches *should* be
   smaller, but not every church *must* be small.
10. Mark Chaves, *American Religion: Contemporary Trends* (Princeton, NJ:
    Princeton University Press, 2011), 124.

11. Eric W. Hayden, "Charles H. Spurgeon: Did You Know?" Christian History, *Christianity Today*, 1991, https://www.christianitytoday.com/history/issues/issue-29/charles-h-spurgeon-did-you-know.html.

12. "Megachurch Definition," Hartford Institute for Religion Research, accessed May 10, 2021, http://hirr.hartsem.edu/megachurch/definition.html. See also "Fast Facts about American Religion," accessed May 10, 2021, http://hirr.hartsem.edu/research/fastfacts/fast_facts.html#numcong.

13. Psalm 117:2.

14. For more on how to create a blue ocean strategy, see W. Chan Kim and Renée Mauborgne, *Blue Ocean Strategy* (Boston: Harvard Business School Publishing, 2015).

15. I recognize the difference between pessimism and cynicism. Pessimists see the worst. Cynics assume that people are motivated by self-interest. It's possible to be a cynic and a leader, but let's be honest: Cynics are no fun to be around and are a real buzzkill.

16. See Thom S. Rainer, *Autopsy of a Deceased Church: 12 Ways to Keep Yours Alive* (Nashville, TN: B&H Publishing Group, 2014); John S. Dickerson, *The Great Evangelical Recession: 6 Factors That Will Crash the American Church . . . and How to Prepare* (Grand Rapids, MI: Baker Books, 2013); David T. Olson, *The American Church in Crisis* (Grand Rapids, MI: Zondervan, 2008).

17. Optimism detached from realism gets weird and kooky. Please don't compare my thoughts to *The Power of Positive Thinking*. You might hurt my feelings.

CHAPTER 1: HIT THE RESET BUTTON, NOT PAUSE

1. See, for example, "Most US Protestant Churches Small with Declining or Stagnant Attendance," Good Faith Media website, March 21, 2019, https://goodfaithmedia.org/most-u-s-protestant-churches-small-with-declining-or-stagnant-attendance/. See also *A Guide to Church Revitalization*, R. Albert Mohler Jr., ed. (Louisville, KY: SBTS Press, 2015), 10.

2. John 14:12.

3. Megan Garber, "Reel Faith: How the Drive-In Movie Theater Helped Create the Megachurch, *The Atlantic*, June 8, 2012, https://www.theatlantic.com/technology/archive/2012/06/reel-faith-how-the-drive-in-movie-theater-helped-create-the-megachurch/258248/.

4. John Markoff, "An Internet Pioneer Ponders the Next Revolution," *New York Times on the Web*, December 20, 1999, https://archive.nytimes.com/www.nytimes.com/library/tech/99/12/biztech/articles/122099outlook-bobb.html?Partner=Snap.

5. Carl Benedikt Frey and Michael Osborne, "Technology at Work: The Future of Innovation and Employment," Citi GPS: Global Perspectives & Solution, February 2015, page 13, https://www.oxfordmartin.ox.ac.uk /downloads/reports/Citi_GPS_Technology_Work.pdf.

6. George E. P. Box and Norman R. Draper, *Empirical Model-Building and Response Surfaces* (New York: John Wiley & Sons, 1987), 424.

7. Bob Dylan, "Blowin' in the Wind," 1962.

8. The following sections are synthesized from several research projects conducted by Church Answers between 2015 and 2020.

9. Lifeway Research, *Becoming Five Multiplication Study: Research Report*, Exponential, February 2019, http://lifewayresearch.com/wp-content /uploads/2019/03/2019ExponentialReport.pdf.

10. See Mark Chaves, *American Religion: Contemporary Trends* (Princeton, NJ: Princeton University Press, 2011).

11. See Dean M. Kelley, *Why Conservative Churches Are Growing* (Macon, GA: Mercer University Press, 1995).

12. Joshua A. Krisch, "Republicans Have More Kids Than Democrats. A Lot More Kids," Yahoo! Finance, March 26, 2019, https://finance.yahoo.com /news/republicans-more-kids-democrats-lot-183722934.html.

13. Thom S. Rainer, "Five Sobering Realities about Evangelism in Our Churches," Church Answers blog, July 10, 2017, https://thomrainer.com /2017/07/five-sobering-realities-evangelism-churches/.

14. *Encyclopaedica Britannica Online*, s.v. "Moore's Law," accessed May 11, 2021, https://www.britannica.com/technology/Moores-law.

15. Felicitie C. Bell and Michael L. Miller, "Life Tables for the United States Social Security Area 1900–2100: Actuarial Study no. 116," Social Security Administration, https://www.ssa.gov/oact/NOTES/as116/as116_V.html. The dip just before 1920 was due to the 1918 flu pandemic, in which many young children perished.

16. Full disclosure: William had also been pushed out of a previous church. But he kept doing what he believed God was calling him to do. Don't ever give up. Jesus didn't. Neither should you.

17. Portions of this section were adapted from Sam Rainer, "Why Every Church Should Move toward Cultural and Racial Diversity," *Leading the Established Church* (blog), May 22, 2016, https://samrainer.com/2016/05 /why-every-church-should-move-toward-cultural-and-racial-diversity/.

18. Paul Taylor, *The Next America: Boomers, Millennials, and the Looming Generational Showdown* (New York: PublicAffairs, 2014, 2015), 16, 23.

19. Jens Manuel Krogstad, "A View of the Nation's Future through Kindergarten Demographics," Pew Research Center, July 31, 2019,

https://www.pewresearch.org/fact-tank/2019/07/31/kindergarten
-demographics-in-us/.

20. Gretchen Livingston and Anna Brown, "Intermarriage in the US 50 Years
    after Loving v. Virginia," Pew Research Center, May 18, 2017, https://
    www.pewsocialtrends.org/2017/05/18/intermarriage-in-the-u-s-50-years
    -after-loving-v-virginia/.

21. Donald A. McGavran, *Understanding Church Growth* (Grand Rapids, MI:
    Eerdmans, 1970), 69.

22. McGavran, *Understanding Church Growth*, x.

23. Bob Smietana, "Research: Racial Diversity at Church More Dream Than
    Reality," Lifeway Research, January 17, 2014, https://lifewayresearch.com
    /2014/01/17/research-racial-diversity-at-church-more-dream-than-reality/.

24. Smietana, "Racial Diversity at Church."

25. Julie Zauzmer, "What Happened When a Black and White Church
    Merged in Florida," *Washington Post*, February 7, 2017, https://
    www.washingtonpost.com/local/social-issues/two-fla-churches--one
    -black-one-white--merge-in-racial-reconciliation-effort/2017/02/07
    /a95dde72-e287-11e6-a547-5fb9411d332c_story.html.

26. Karl Vaters, "14 Observations about the State of Christian Denominations
    Today," *Pivot*, a blog of *Christianity Today*, April 15, 2019, https://
    www.christianitytoday.com/karl-vaters/2019/april/christian-denominations
    -today.html.

27. Paul A. Djupe, "Why We Should Worry about the Decline of
    Denominationalism (in the US)," Religion in Public, May 4, 2017,
    https://religioninpublic.blog/2017/05/04/decline-of-denominationalism/.

CHAPTER 2: THE REVITALIZATION CHECKLIST

1. This chapter was inspired by Atul Gawande's book *The Checklist Manifesto:
   How to Get Things Right* (New York: Picador, 2010). I encourage you to get
   a copy of the book and read it carefully.

2. Credit for this concept again goes to Atul Gawande. Read his book.

3. Karl Vaters, *The Church Recovery Guide: How Your Congregation Can Adapt
   and Thrive after a Crisis* (Chicago: Moody, 2020), 31.

4. See, for example, Brian Croft, *Biblical Church Revitalization: Solutions for
   Dying and Divided Churches* (Fearn, Scotland: Christian Focus, 2020), a
   small book that answers several key questions relative to the revitalization
   process. See also Andrew M. Davis, *Revitalize: Biblical Keys to Helping Your
   Church Come Alive Again* (Grand Rapids, MI: Baker, 2017), an excellent
   resource to provide spiritual help for pastors leading struggling churches.
   The thrust of Davis's book is more spiritual than practical.

5. See Mark Clifton, *Reclaiming Glory: Revitalizing Dying Churches* (Nashville, TN: B&H Books, 2016). This book is considered the seminal work on church replanting. It is an inspiring must-read for all pastors leading revitalization work.

6. This research was conducted in 2020 within the Church Answers community and through social media.

7. Thom S. Rainer, "Hope for Dying Churches," Lifeway Research, January 16, 2018, https://lifewayresearch.com/2018/01/16/hope-for-dying-churches/.

CHAPTER 3: PRIORITIES

1. See Donald A. McGavran, *Understanding Church Growth* (Grand Rapids, MI: Eerdmans, 1985), 24.

2. Ephesians 4:12.

3. Portions of this section were adapted from Sam Rainer, "Be the Church that Embraces Children, Not Just Tolerates Them," *Leading the Established Church* (blog), April 7, 2019, https://samrainer.com/?s=Embrace+Children%2C+Don%E2%80%99t+Just+Tolerate+Them.

4. Matthew 28:20.

CHAPTER 4: PACE

1. Carl George names this phenomenon the Berry-Bucket Theory in Carl F. George and Robert E. Logan, *Leading and Managing Your Church* (Grand Rapids, MI: Revell, 1988), chapter 10. It's an oldie but goodie.

2. Jim Collins, *Good to Great: Why Some Companies Make the Leap . . . and Others Don't* (New York: HarperBusiness, 2001), 164.

3. Collins, *Good to Great*, 14, 164–165.

4. Thom S. Rainer, *Breakout Churches: Discover How to Make the Leap* (Grand Rapids, MI: Zondervan, 2005), 165–184.

5. National Center for Health Statistics, "Deaths and Mortality," Centers for Disease Control and Prevention, last reviewed April 9, 2021, https://www.cdc.gov/nchs/fastats/deaths.htm.

6. For a discussion of "change or die," see the concluding chapter in Thom S. Rainer, *Anatomy of a Revived Church: Seven Findings of How Congregations Avoided Death* (Spring Hill, TN: Rainer Publishing, 2020).

CHAPTER 5: PERSPECTIVE

1. Matthew 14:24-26; Mark 6:47-50.

2. Andrew M. Davis, *Revitalize: Biblical Keys to Helping Your Church Come Alive Again* (Grand Rapids, MI: Baker Books, 2017), 170.

3. Davis, *Revitalize*, 172.
4. See Thom S. Rainer, *High Expectations: The Remarkable Secret for Keeping People in Your Church* (Nashville, TN: B&H Books, 1999).
5. In another conversation early in our marriage, my wife informed me she would move with me anywhere but Florida. We now live in Bradenton and she loves it.
6. Sam S. Rainer III, "Legacy Church Leadership in the Southern Baptist Convention" (doctoral dissertation, Dallas Baptist University, May 2017).
7. 2 Kings 14:25.
8. Jonah 1:1-3.

CHAPTER 6: PEOPLE
1. Haggai 2:19.
2. James 1:12.
3. Haggai 1:2.
4. Haggai 1:3-15.
5. When trying to understand how a church business meeting went sideways on you, Ezra 3:10-13 is about as descriptive an Old Testament text as you will find.
6. Credit goes to Andrew Davis for the term "double agents." See Andrew M. Davis, *Revitalize: Biblical Keys to Helping Your Church Come Alive Again* (Grand Rapids, MI: Baker Books, 2017), 17.
7. Brad Bitterly and Alison Wood Brooks, "Sarcasm, Self-Deprecation, and Inside Jokes: A User's Guide to Humor at Work," *Harvard Business Review*, July–August 2020, https://hbr.org/2020/07/sarcasm-self-deprecation-and-inside-jokes-a-users-guide-to-humor-at-work.
8. "Expect Great Things; Attempt Great Things," Center for Study of the Life and Work of William Carey, D.D. (1761–1834), https://www.wmcarey.edu/carey/expect/expect.htm.
9. William Carey, quoted in Mark Galli, "The Man Who Wouldn't Give Up," Christian History Institute, accessed May 19, 2021, https://christianhistoryinstitute.org/magazine/article/man-who-would-not-give-up.
10. Carey, in "The Man Who Wouldn't Give Up."
11. Haggai 2:9.

CHAPTER 7: PLACE
1. See Timothy A. Songster, *Healthy Church by Design: The Synergy between Buildings and Church Health* (Spring Hill, TN: Rainer Publishing, 2018).
2. See Tim Cool, *Why Church Buildings Matter: The Story of Your Space* (Spring Hill, TN: Rainer Publishing, 2017).

3. See Lee G. Bolman and Terrence E. Deal, *Reframing Organizations: Artistry, Choice, and Leadership* (San Francisco: Jossey-Bass, 2008).

4. Cyndi Richardson, *By His Grace and for His Glory* (Cordova, TN: Bellevue Baptist Church, 2003), 243.

5. I developed this thought in depth in my dissertation on legacy churches. See Sam S. Rainer III, "Legacy Church Leadership in the Southern Baptist Convention" (doctoral dissertation, Dallas Baptist University, May 2017).

6. "Sputnik and the Dawn of the Space Age," NASA History Division, accessed May 19, 2021, https://history.nasa.gov/sputnik/.

7. Tariq Malik, "NASA's Space Shuttle by the Numbers: 30 Years of a Spaceflight Icon," Space.com, accessed May 19, 2021, https://www.space.com/12376-nasa-space-shuttle-program-facts-statistics.html.

8. See Ed Stetzer and Daniel Im, *Planting Missional Churches: Your Guide to Starting Churches That Multiply* (Nashville, TN: B&H Books, 2016).

9. *Force majeure* is a term used in contracts to refer to unforeseeable circumstances that prevent one or multiple parties from fulfilling stipulated obligations. The phrase technically means "superior force" but is often stated as "an act of God."

10. "Storm History," in "Catastrophic Hurricane Michael Strikes Florida Panhandle, October 10, 2018," National Weather Service, https://www.weather.gov/tae/HurricaneMichael2018.

11. The original research was conducted in 2008 by Rainer Research, now part of Church Answers.

12. "Let us not neglect our meeting together, *as some people do*, but encourage one another, especially now that the day of his return is drawing near" (Hebrews 10:25, emphasis added).

CHAPTER 8: PURPOSE

1. A 2019 Lifeway Research survey found that, over a six-month period, only 45 percent of active churchgoers shared their faith. See Aaron Earls, "Evangelism More Prayed For than Practiced by Churchgoers," Lifeway Research, April 23, 2019, https://lifewayresearch.com/2019/04/23/evangelism-more-prayed-for-than-practiced-by-churchgoers/.

2. This formula first appeared in Thom S. Rainer, *Surprising Insights from the Unchurched and Proven Ways to Reach Them* (Grand Rapids, MI: Zondervan, 2001). The original formula used membership as the numerator rather than average weekly attendance. However, membership is no longer considered a reliable metric due to the inflated nature of membership rolls in many church databases.

3. Thom S. Rainer, *The Post-Quarantine Church: Six Urgent Challenges and*

Opportunities That Will Determine the Future of Your Congregation (Carol
Stream, IL: Tyndale Momentum, 2020), 39.

4. Cynthia Woolever and Deborah Bruce, *A Field Guide to US Congregations:
Who's Going Where and Why* (Louisville, KY: Westminster John Knox Press,
2010), 27.

5. Matthew 28:19-20.

CHAPTER 9: PATHWAY

1. The MHAG was inspired by Jim Collins's "big hairy audacious goal"
(BHAG), which he introduced in his classic management book, *Good
to Great*. Collins suggests the NASA moon mission of the 1960s as
an example of a BHAG. The MHAG was developed by my father,
Thom S. Rainer, and the Church Answers team. We use it in our micro
consultations.

2. D. A. Carson, *For the Love of God: A Daily Companion for Discovering the
Riches of God's Word*, volume 2 (Wheaton, IL: Crossway, 1999), reading
for January 23.

3. Adapted from Sabina Nawaz, "For Delegation to Work, It Has to
Come with Coaching," *Harvard Business Review*, May 5, 2016, https://
hbr.org/2016/05/for-delegation-to-work-it-has-to-come-with-coaching.

4. See James M. Kouzes and Barry Z. Posner, *A Leader's Legacy* (San Francisco:
Jossey-Bass, 2006).

5. This idea comes from one of my mentors, Brad Waggoner. He challenged
me to rethink the way I communicate, both personally and professionally.

CHAPTER 10: COMPLETING YOUR CHURCH REVITALIZATION CHECKLIST

1. Ezekiel 37:4-6.

2. We recommend ChurchHealthReport.com.

3. We recommend the Know Your Community report, which can be found
at ChurchAnswers.com/solutions/tools/.

4. Check out the Pray and Go resource at ChurchAnswers.com/course
/pray-and-go/.

5. Isaiah 43:7.

About the Author

SAM RAINER serves as president of Church Answers and is a cofounder of Rainer Publishing. He is also lead pastor at West Bradenton Baptist Church in Bradenton, Florida. He writes, teaches, speaks, and consults on a variety of church health issues. Sam cohosts the popular podcasts *Rainer on Leadership* and *EST.church*.

Sam is the author of *Obstacles in the Established Church* and the coauthor of *Essential Church?* He has written hundreds of articles for several publications and is a frequent conference speaker on church health issues.

Sam holds a BS in finance and marketing from the University of South Carolina, an MA in missiology from Southern Seminary, and a PhD in leadership studies from Dallas Baptist University. He resides in Bradenton, Florida, with his wife and four children. The Rainers are also a foster family, so it's likely there are more kids in the house at any given time. They have a dog and a cat that his daughters insisted on keeping.

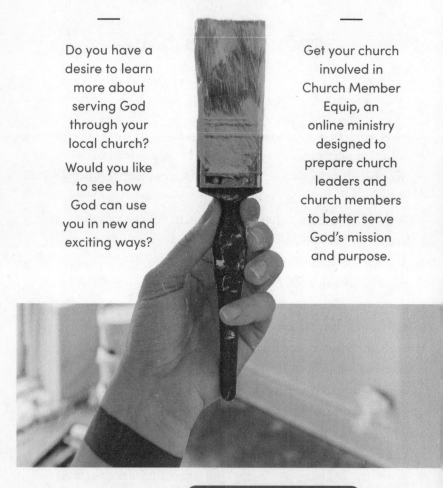